revealing JEWEL
an INTIMATE portrait from FAMILY AND friends

With Introductions by Atz Lee Kilcher

Edited by Kenneth Calhoun and Cambria Jensen

D1377897

ATRIA BOOKS

New York   London   Toronto   Sydney   Singapore

ATRIA BOOKS
1230 Avenue of the Americas
New York, NY 10020

ISBN: 0-7434-7540-2

First Atria Books trade paperback edition June 2003

10 9 8 7 6 5 4 3 2 1

ATRIA BOOKS is a trademark of Simon & Schuster, Inc.

Manufactured in the United States of America

For information regarding special discounts for bulk purchases, please contact
Simon & Schuster Special Sales at 1-800-456-6798 or business@simonandschuster.com

CREDITS & ACKNOWLEDGMENTS

Interviews by Kenneth Calhoun.
Brady Blade interview by Anna Bissell.

Book design and production by Berne Smith.

Cover photograph and Jewel Q & A photograph by Troy Jensen.
All other photographs by West Kennerly.

Special thanks to the many individuals who agreed to be interviewed for this book.
Their collective voices made this project possible.

Thank you also to those fans who submitted questions for Jewel, some of which were
used in the Jewel Q & A segments appearing throughout this book.

NOTE: Some of the names of persons appearing in this book have been changed in order to protect their privacy.

Visit Jewel's website: www.jeweljk.com

The goal of this book is to provide a complete picture of Jewel—one of the most original, and complicated, personalities in today's music world. Meeting this objective proved to be a bit of a challenge. Jewel is many different things to many different people. For example, some are drawn to her vulnerability, her sweetness, while others relate to her as a tough-as-nails survivor. To some, she's a down-to-earth, outdoorsy type, at ease in natural settings. Yet others see her as sophisticated and glamorous. Of course, Jewel is all of these things (and more). Our challenge was to find a way to capture these many facets of her character and present them as a unified, true portrait of the artist.

After considering a number of possible formats, we settled on a book of interviews and photographs. The photos would speak for themselves, showing Jewel in a variety of settings, situations and moods. But what about the interviews? The obvious choice was to talk to key people in her life and then present their comments in sections organized by topic. This is essentially what we've done, but rather than limit a page or idea to one voice, we thought it would be cool to hear from a number of voices on any given topic.

What we ended up with is a format that looks more like a panel discussion or, to put it more plainly, a conversation. But these conversations didn't start out as such—they were pieced together after we interviewed everyone individually. This might seem like a strange way to do things, but we had our reasons. For one thing, it gave us more control over the flow of the conversation and we could really explore things more deeply when dealing with people one-on-one. Another concern was a basic music biz reality: Getting all these people to sit around the table at the same time would have been a scheduling and logistical nightmare.

Cool things started happening immediately as we began putting the conversations together. There was a natural flow to each discussion, since people had some shared experiences to draw from. They validated and reinforced what others had said without even knowing it. There were also some intriguing contradictions that spoke volumes about Jewel's multifaceted nature.

We let the conversations go where they wanted to, then dropped in some longer quotes by her more famous friends and collaborators. Then we rounded the whole thing out with some input from Jewel herself, getting her response to more than a few pointed questions. The final product, which you now hold in your hand, took two years to put together and is comprised of more than thirty voices and dozens of never-before-seen photos. In reading it, you'll go beyond all the superficial media impressions and into Jewel's true character in a way that most artists wouldn't even allow.

Of course, no book can capture the entirety of a personality or a life—especially when we're talking about someone as unique as Jewel. But if you really want to know what Jewel's truly like, beyond what this book or any other book can tell you, beyond even knowing her personally, try this: *Listen closely to her music*. Ultimately, as with all great artists, it's through her art that Jewel reveals her truest self.

The Editors

Before his untimely death in May 2002, Kevyn was one of the most sought-after makeup artists in the world. His clients included Julia Roberts, Tori Amos, Gwyneth Paltrow, Winona Ryder and Britney Spears. He has written three books on the art of makeup, including *Making Faces* and the best-seller *Face Forward*. Kevyn and Jewel first met when he volunteered to do her makeup for a *Late Show with David Letterman* appearance.

Kevyn Aucoin
makeup artist

A longtime member of the Jewel team, Alan has the formidable task of archiving all of Jewel's recordings, which includes performances, raw demos and studio recordings. He also plays the role of chief liaison between the Jewel team and Jewel's fan base.

Alan Bershaw
archive manager

Bibi toured extensively with Jewel, often videotaping their travels. She coproduced *Jewel: A Life Uncommon*, a documentary video.

Bibi
friend, videographer

Brady met Jewel when he was playing with Emmylou Harris (Lilith Fair Tour 1997). He has also played with Steve Earle.

Brady Blade
Spirit Tour drummer

A longtime family friend, Brandon accompanied Jewel on the Spirit and This Way Tours.

Brandon
friend

Lenedra is an artist, poet, entrepreneur, author, singer and philanthropist. In 2001, she published her first book, *The Architecture of All Abundance*.

Lenedra J. Carroll
Jewel's mother and manager

Darren videotaped Jewel throughout the Spirit Tour. He continues to work with Jewel, documenting live appearances and fan interactions.

Darren
videographer

As Jewel's acting agent from 1995 to 1996, Michael introduced Jewel to a variety of directors and others in the entertainment industry. As Jewel's friend, he has accompanied her to numerous celebrity gatherings and high-profile events.

Michael Davis
Jewel's former acting agent

Steve George Spirit Tour & This Way Tour keyboardist	Besides being a key member of Mister Mister in the 1980s, Steve has toured with Kenny Loggins.
Trey Gray This Way Tour drummer	A Nashville session man, Trey has also played with Faith Hill.
T-Bone Hannon This Way Tour bassist	Prior to touring with Jewel, T-Bone played bass for gospel greats Bebe and Cece Winans, as well as Amy Grant, Michael W. Smith and SheDaisy.
Dann Huff producer	Dann built a reputation as a session guitarist, playing on tracks for the likes of Barbra Streisand, Reba McEntire, Celine Dion and Rod Stewart. As a producer, he has worked with Megadeth and Faith Hill, among others. He was paired with Jewel to produce the song "Till We Run Out of Road" and was asked to coproduce all of *This Way* with Jewel.
Atz Kilcher Singer/songwriter, Jewel's father	Atz has written and performed songs his entire life. His talent for engaging the audience and delivering moving concerts has greatly shaped Jewel's performance style. His latest CD, *Spirit-Filled Air*, was released in 2000.
Atz Lee Kilcher Jewel's younger brother	Atz Lee presently lives in Homer, Alaska, near the homestead where he, Jewel and Shane were raised.
Shane Kilcher Jewel's older brother	Shane is the cultural specialist and assistant director for The ClearWater Project, which is the flagship endeavor of Jewel and Lenedra Carroll's humanitarian foundation, Higher Ground for Humanity.
Daniel Lanois producer, friend	Daniel was called the "most important record producer to emerge in the Eighties" by *Rolling Stone*. He has produced acclaimed albums by U2, Bob Dylan, Peter Gabriel, Emmylou Harris and many others. A guitarist and songwriter, his solo projects are *Acadie* and *For the Beauty of Wynona*. Daniel first met Jewel in San Diego, when he decided to investigate industry buzz on "this great folksinger."
Lee friend	A resident of Homer, Alaska, Lee toured with Jewel as a companion and helped in all sorts of ways.
Patrick Leonard producer	A songwriter, musician and producer, Patrick has worked with Madonna, Roger Waters and Elton John. In 2000, he

released a CD of his own compositions called *Rivers*. He produced *Spirit* and cowrote "Hands" with Jewel.

The legendary Arif Mardin, producer of the Grammy-winning Norah Jones CD, *Come Away with Me*, is considered one of the most important producers of the 20th century. He is especially recognized for his work with the great female vocalists, such as Barbra Streisand, Bette Midler and Whitney Houston. He produced *Joy* for Jewel in 1999.

Arif Mardin
producer

A songwriter and lead guitarist, Stuart has played for numerous acts, including Lifehouse. He recently released a CD of original material called *Pathetic Love Songs* and, as a solo artist, opened for Jewel's 2002 New Wild West Tour.

Stuart Mathis
This Way Tour guitarist

In 2002, Moby released *18*, the follow-up CD to his critical and commercial breakthrough, *Play* (1999). An influential figure in today's music scene, Moby is an innovator of electronic music and a devout Christian and vegan. His eclectic Area Music Festival has toured two consecutive summers to great acclaim. He met Jewel in England, when both were featured guests on *Top of the Pops*.

Moby
musician, friend

Monty met Jewel on her first tour, when she served as the opening act for Peter Murphy. He has managed every Jewel tour since.

Monty
tour manager

Often referred to as the "King of the Cowboys" or the "Michael Jordan of Rodeo," Ty is the most accomplished athlete in the history of the sport, with nine world titles to his name. Ty and Jewel met at a rodeo in Denver, when Jewel was touring in the area.

Ty Murray
champion bullrider, boyfriend

A veteran songwriter, Rick has cowritten songs with Madonna, k.d. lang, Celine Dion and others. He cowrote the music for "Standing Still," "This Way" and "I Won't Walk Away," from the *This Way* album.

Rick Nowels
songwriter/producer

Based in Nashville, Mark has played with Martina McBride, Amy Grant and Dann Huff.

Mark Oakley
This Way Tour guitarist

Since the Spirit World Tour, Doug has toured with Tracy Chapman and Lucinda Williams.

Doug Pettibone
Spirit Tour guitarist

Steve Poltz Spirit Tour rhythm guitarist, friend	A longtime friend, Steve is a fixture of the San Diego music scene as a member of the Rugburns and an accomplished solo artist. He and Jewel have cowritten numerous songs, including "You Were Meant for Me." He has toured extensively with Jewel, often serving as both the opening act and Jewel's rhythm guitarist.
Sharon friend	As Jewel's "road mom" and close friend, Sharon acted as an assistant during the Spirit Tour.
Stephen assistant	Stephen functions as a liaison between Jewel and management, particularly when Jewel is traveling.
Billy Bob Thornton actor, director, musician, friend	Academy Award–winner Billy Bob wrote, starred in and directed *Sling Blade* and played lead roles in *Pushing Tin*, *The Man Who Wasn't There* and *Monster's Ball*. In the fall of 2001, he released a CD titled *Private Radio*. He met Jewel while directing *All the Pretty Horses*, when Jewel was visiting some cowboy friends on the set.
West Jewel's official photographer	West took an interest in Jewel when she was a rising star of the San Diego coffeehouse scene. He is the only photographer Jewel will invite into casual, behind-the-scenes settings.

My sister loves Alaska; she feels a deep connection with the land that raised her and the people that had an impact on her early years. But I suppose that is what most people would feel towards a place where they were raised by a pack of wolves on an 8,000-acre arctic mountain range without food, running water or any contact with the outside world, other than the weekly yodeling report from the neighboring mountain peaks—or so the story goes.

Since Jewel's rise to fame, her background has been at times as much of a source of entertainment as her music. And some of the stories that have been spun out of a few bits of truth are just as creative as her songs. People seem to be truly interested in where she came from and what she was like prior to being a rock star. But finding answers from a reliable source has proven to be as challenging as getting Jewel to stand still long enough to catch up with her. In this section, we explore what stands out foremost in the minds of those who knew Jewel before stardom. It's as straight a scoop as could be found, and it has yet to be seen whether it cuts through the mythology or just adds to it.

Similar to our grandfather, who set out towards an unknown land in hopes of a better life, Jewel left Alaska and the familiarities of home. People that leave a place where all their roots are, and set out for a new sense of life and accomplishment, are the modern-day pioneers. Jewel fits the description. But her story doesn't start with leaving home. As you'll see, things had been building for quite some time, starting way back when, as kids, we performed as a family. If she hadn't left, she'd probably still be singing, still creating, no matter what her setting. But it was leaving that gave the story a chance to grow into what it is.

When all's said and done, Jewel is just another person raised in these strange times we live in. There is nothing different about her besides the fact that she focused extremely hard on her dreams and managed to manifest them into everyday life. Something anyone is capable of doing; it just takes faith and focus. Jewel knew this. Or if she didn't when she started out, she knows it now. And maybe by reading this others will know it to be true in terms of their own lives.

Atz Lee Kilcher

Atz Lee Homer has changed a lot, as all small towns do. It kind of took off as a place for people that didn't want to be called hippies. People who wanted to go somewhere else, where they could live off the land and not worry about whether or not they looked like everyone else. They came up here to have a self-sufficient lifestyle.

Before that, like with our parents' parents, the homesteaders in the '40s, there were a lot of people who were out for a new way of life—kind of the same thing, only these were Europeans, and mixed ethnicities. People that wanted to start a new something—a new way of life, a new community, a new family. Break away from old traditions.

This Way Tour, Orlando, FL, 6/16/02

Lee It's a small town, Homer, but you would be surprised at all the cool people that live there.

West The people are really charming. I got a strong sense of community when I went up there. I saw how that could have affected Jewel. But having said that, I could also see where that environment could be very confining, and I could see how she would have thrived coming to San Diego from that kind of environment. She could blossom here because the possibilities are limitless, for a young person having grown up in such a remote area.

The whole bay area, Kachemak Bay, is physically stunning, just beautiful to look at. Jewel's very much at home in that rugged environment. You can tell when you're up there with her that it's her church.

Sharon In living the life she did, in nature, in solitude, there's a pureness, a lack of pretense to her now. She draws a lot from that.

Where was Jewel born?

Utah

a FAMILY entertainment show

Shane My mom and dad had two albums out, and they were really well known in the community—both very outgoing, affable people. They had a family entertainment show, and we were all part of it.

Alan Her father, Atz, is a great storyteller. And he's someone who takes being a professional musician very seriously, and I think he instilled that work ethic in Jewel.

Lee I had just moved up to Homer from Los Angeles when they were performing a lot as a family. Someone told me, "There's an event going on at

Can you imagine yourself living somewhere other than the U.S.?

I was never tremendously patriotic until I left the States. America really has a way of life that spoils you for anything else, I think. I really enjoy supermarkets—I know that sounds silly. But you just get really used to Japanese, Chinese, Mexican or Italian on any given evening. The only other country I really fell in love with and thought I could spend time there, like as a summer home, is Italy.

Land's End [a tourist resort]. The Kilchers are performing." Jewel was really the highlight of the show, but it was, honestly, one of the best musical events that I had seen in a long time, and I was coming right out of the music scene in L.A.

I had a couple days off that I had planned to go on a camping trip with this ol' guy that's a friend of mine from California. We were going to go up into the Sierra Nevadas and camp and fish, and we were going to pack in there on horseback. I had already kind of had that planned with him for a while. So Jewel and I were wanting to see each other, and I didn't have any days off other than that. I said to her, "Well, I'm going on a fishing trip up into the mountains with this ol' friend of mine. He's a really cool guy. You want to go?" And she said, "Sure."

I didn't know anything about her background—where she was raised—and I wasn't real sure about taking her, you know. We were on horses, and we were going to ride up into those mountains and sleep on the ground and fish, cook on the campfire and all this.

"Well, we'll see what she's MADE of."

I joked with Pat—the guy I was going up there with—I said, "I'm going to take this girl I met." I said, "I don't know how well she's going to do, but I told her what we're going to do and she said she'd like to go."

He said, "Well, we'll see what she's made of." Anyway, we took her and she got along real good. I didn't know if she had ever been on a horse.

The funny part of the story is, later on, when I went with her to Alaska and saw where she was raised, and saw the cabin she grew up in and all that, I felt it was pretty funny thinking she might not be able to handle that camping trip.

It's real rugged up there. The cabin on the homestead that she grew up in is rustic like nobody would ever be able to understand.

Ty Murray

Lenedra   Jewel was very shy as a young child, so I was surprised when she said she wanted to sing with her father and me. I remember the first time she got on stage and she just took to it. It was a very noticeable thing. She just seemed to know how to do it. She enjoyed the crowd and played to the crowd immediately.

Atz Lee   We were all somewhat shy. It just depended on the situation. If we were in a store or at somebody's house, we were usually shy and kind of held back. But if we were onstage, we had a tendency to lean the other way. I mean, we would start off shy, with maybe the first few songs, then we'd warm up into ourselves. That's one of the reasons we liked music and wanted to be involved in our parents' music, because we could feel that looseness come to us as we started singing it.

Shane   I really couldn't deal well with my dad saying, "You didn't hit that note." That was kind of it for me. But Jewel stuck with it. She thrives on a challenge, especially if it's a matter of internal resources. She just knows she can muster whatever it's going to require.

Lee   She used to come to my cabin before it was finished, when it only had three walls, and she'd go upstairs and play. At the time it was just a big opening where the wall should be. I'd be out working in the garden, and friends would come and visit. They thought I had a stereo on. Her singing was ringing out over the fields. They would hear her from the garden and say, "Where did you get this music? What is going on?"

I'd say, "No. That's my friend Jewel. She's upstairs in the house, singing."

Shane   We didn't have much to do. Most of our lives, for example, we didn't have television. Whether it's because we were bored or whatever, she would sit in front of the mirror for hours and practice moving different facial muscles. She still has a lot of facial muscle control. She can twitch the eye muscle in her lower eyelid of her left eye. It's pretty cool. It sounds kind of funny, but it's really a good example of her self-control. She just knows she can do it.

We really grew up believing that, if being a successful artist is what you wanted to do, you could. If you committed yourself to doing it, you could do it. Jewel was able to focus on the things she wanted, and they would happen.

What was the name of Jewel's childhood horse?

Clearwater

Of all your jobs, which was the crappiest?

I worked in a computer warehouse that sold computer chips and software. I was just answering the phones. I didn't have it long. That's the famous job I got fired from that caused me to move into my van. My boss was being . . . unprofessional. I've really never had a boss that didn't try to screw me. [laughter]

Was the Interlochen fund-raiser show a pivotal event in your life?

Absolutely. That fund-raising concert was a great experience. The whole town turned out to support me in my dream. It was really humbling, and to this day it's a reminder of how profound a sense of community can be. Many people—people who didn't have to—came together to help me. It is part of the reason why I feel so strongly about giving back.

It's funny to hear that people thought, back then, that I'd go places. I sure didn't. I wasn't sure I'd get to Interlochen. Getting to that school was my only goal.

Lee   I have friends that I wrote letters to in those early years, and they've called me recently saying, "I just found this letter and in it you're talking about your friend Jewel, saying she's going to be famous." She was like 16 at the time. At first, she was maybe embarrassed by her age. I don't think she lied to me, but she just didn't tell me she was that young.

She lived on her own then, and she was very independent. She was talking about going to this school, Interlochen.

Lenedra   When Jewel heard there was a school that focused on art as well as academics she was very excited to go, because high school had felt like a waste of time to her. The thought of being able to study music and explore other kinds of art—dance, sculpture, drama, painting—sounded perfect to her because she had so many passions.

Shane   She still had the mind frame of "I could kind of live an artsy life if I want to." She thought she could sing for a living somehow. It's a really cool thing to go to school to do.

Lee   She really wanted to go. There was this whole issue: She needed to raise money. She put on this show to raise the tuition for Interlochen. She had these posters made. She went around and put them up, and she went around soliciting. I mean, she was really working hard. She had drive. She wanted to go somewhere and that was really evident.

Shane   I didn't have a real clear impression that she would be famous, or that music is what she would do. Not until I think she was getting ready to go to Interlochen, after she had just turned 16. Then she and some family members and friends put on the fund-raiser, and the city of Homer came and basically funded her going to Interlochen.

Lee Everyone that came was amazed. I brought a lot of people, saying, "This is the girl I've been talking about." After the show, people's eyes were wide open. They could only say, "Wow." But they'd say it three times because they just didn't know how to express their amazement. "Wow, wow, wow."

Shane To see her doing the show—I hadn't seen her for a while, so it was a fresh perspective. And also she had really grown and developed while I was away at school. And to see the changes in her, and to see from a new perspective, I realized then: "Wow, she can really do whatever she wants." She had a fabulous voice, and she was writing some good stuff. That was where I thought she's really got the potential to do it all.

Pre-show, This Way Tour, Cleveland, OH, 7/7/02

Lenedra Jewel met Flea from the Red Hot Chili Peppers at a health institute in San Diego before she even began to pursue her career. She was sitting out on the curb in the parking lot with her guitar, playing, and this guy came up and said, "You have a great voice."

They struck up a conversation. He asked whose song it was that she was playing and she said it was hers. He said, "That's a really great song. Do you have any others?"

So she started playing songs for him. He was the first celebrity musician that Jewel met and certainly the first that she played songs for. He really encouraged her to do something with her music. Their friendship stems from those days, just as she started singing in the coffeehouses.

When Jewel was fourteen, who was she adopted by?

An Ottawa Indian tribe

West I was just going from coffeehouse to coffeehouse seeing what was going on. At that time in San Diego, there was a lot of good music in coffeehouses. But Jewel just stood out. You could tell, even at that early stage, that she was going places. And I would always make a special effort to be at the InnerChange on Thursday nights.

Bibi I met Jewel at the InnerChange Coffeehouse. Some friends of mine lived a few blocks away, and they had started going every Thursday night to see her and they were trying to convince me to go. And probably after the tenth time of them saying, "You gotta check this out," I went and saw her set.

I'm like, "Well, she's good."

She sang a song in Swedish and I speak Swedish, so after the show I went up to talk to her in Swedish. Then I discovered that she only knew ten words of Swedish, the ten words that were in her song. We had a little laugh over it.

Alan She came back to San Diego in '92, after Interlochen. At first she was wait-ressing, but she did start doing sporadic gigs, like Steve Poltz would invite her up to do a couple of songs during his sets. So her coffeehouse days really, as far as San Diego is concerned, are from late '92 to early '94—so there's almost a year and a half there.

That whole InnerChange time that's so famous really was approximately a year. It was a very brief time. She was doing other coffeehouses in the area, but she had a regular gig at the InnerChange that would just build and build and build.

Bibi   When I started going, you would have to show up about an hour before her show. Then it got to the point where if you wanted to get into the 9:00 show, you had to be there in time for the 7:00 show to stand in line. You'd be standing outside while she was doing her show. She played two shows every Thursday night. Sometimes the late show went for four hours.

Shane   Really, overall, from the time she decided to sing until she was kind of sensational was really a short period of time. One day she was working odd jobs and the next she was getting paid for playing her music.

The word on the street at the time was that there was a great folksinger playing at one of these little San Diego coffeehouses. I made my way there. I was, in fact, doing some surfing in the area anyhow. So I decided I'd stop in and check her out. And, sure enough, she was great: beautiful voice and just something very innocent and powerful about her presence. So I was there for the whole show, and we hung out a bit afterwards and, well, had some burritos. She was just learning how to surf then, and this was good timing because I was able to give her a few tips on board maintenance, and I think her surfing surely improved after my presence. [laughter]

There were some folks coming around. The word was out, but she was not signed to Atlantic at the time. There was talk of me making the record, but it just didn't work out because I got busy. Plus, I thought a little folksy record like that could never sell. [laughter] That's not true. I knew she had a very good chance. There were some cynics out there. I remember having a conversation with a few of my buddies in the industry: "No, no. She's not ready."

"She is ready! She's great!"

"She IS ready! She's GREAT!"

She's a storyteller. She's gifted with that beautiful voice, and she can write lovely melodies. I think that's what's going to survive the tidal wave of constant change. Whether we're going through hip-hop, country or rock. I think there's a very, very large chunk of the world that likes clarity in a song and melody. She has that. She can enjoy whatever kind of framing she likes, as long as the center never changes.

Daniel Lanois

Bibi   I went a few more times to see her at the InnerChange and we started talking. Then I found out I was moving into a little studio apartment in a canyon in Hillcrest, San Diego, and she lived right across the canyon from me.

Who was your first love?

My first serious boyfriend was a Swedish guy. I was 18. He was in his early 20s. We were pretty serious. We drove across the country together in his car. He was going to come down to San Diego and live with me when I ended up in my van. He was going to live in my van with me! And then I realized there were two paths I could take: marriage or focus on myself. I decided to focus on myself, and that was one very shocked 24-year-old guy.

Somehow I told her I was moving and she told me where she lived, and sure enough, it was the street right across from mine, with a view of my tiny little studio. She lived in a house that was right across the canyon, and she had obviously already gotten her advance from the record deal because it was a pretty nice house. Not amazing, but still better than what I had as a little college student. She converted the balcony to a bedroom, enclosed with just a screen. I could hear her singing and playing her guitar, writing new songs. I remember hearing her write a song early one morning. It woke me up, and then that night she performed it for the first time at the InnerChange.

Once I found out we were neighbors, we just became friends. And then I met her mother, Lenedra. We just started going to have tea or coffee.

Alan When I first got interested in Jewel, just for the hell of it, I contacted every sound guy I knew and asked if they had ever mixed a club show for this girl Jewel. At that time, her album wasn't moving. She had done the residency tour thing and then played all these ding-dong one-off places, so I thought at least a couple of my friends had mixed sound for her at one time or another.

Surprisingly, there were many of them that had mixed for her. I repeatedly asked, "Did you happen to make a tape?" And the mindblower was that they all had the same story. They all basically said, "Yeah, I have a tape, but the first two or three songs are missing." All of these guys told me the same story.

The reason was that they had no idea who she was and expected nothing. It was just some folksinger chick showing up

Where does the title of Jewel's book, *Chasing Down the Dawn*, come from?

Her poem "The Slow Migration of Glaciers"

and they're mixing for her. And they would get the mix set and be all ho-hum about it. Then they'd start listening to her and go, "Wow, she's really good." And that's when they'd pop the tape in and begin recording.

Pre-show, This Way Tour, Vienna, VA, 6/19/02

Shane   Once she decided that's what she really wanted to do, and went for it, Atlantic gave her a small advance, and she used it to help pay rent on a new place. And to buy a car. I think she bought Mom a car, too. But it's like, what did they get? You'd think they'd get something cool. They both got used Volvos.

We're a thrifty, practical family. She'd been living in a van and the van was dying. It wasn't running anymore and they needed another car. And the Volvo's a really good, reliable car. Its titanium alloy, high-tension steel frame protects you in accidents up to 120 miles per hour. Buy one now. [laughter]

Pre-show, This Way Tour, Boston, MA, 6/23/02

Lenedra   When Jewel got her advance check from her record deal, she wanted to put it in the bank and not spend anything. I had to talk her into getting a place to live and a used car. She didn't really have either of those things. But she was convinced that the advance might be the only money she would ever make, and she wanted to save it. Jewel continues to be very frugal and prudent in her spending. It's a basic personality trait.

PAYING HERdues

Alan   I first saw her in 1995. She was part of a festival in Hartford, Connecticut. It was a radio station festival where there were all these alternative bands and

Jewel. She really didn't fit in at all. It was just her, alone onstage, with just a guitar. I remember seeing her there so well, because she literally looked like she was 12 years old. She was wearing a Pink Panther T-shirt. When she first started, nobody was paying attention to her at all. About halfway through her set, people began taking notice. And by the end, people were just dumbstruck.

Bibi   Jewel and I went up to L.A. for a photo shoot, and we were driving home late at night. She had rented a car from, literally, Rent-A-Wreck. Both our cars were in the shop or something. So we were driving home in this Rent-A-Wreck, and her song came on. It was "Who Will Save Your Soul."

I hadn't heard it before, so it was really my very first time. But she recognized it right off the bat, and she was screaming and hitting me and saying, "OH MY GOD, THIS IS MY SONG! THIS IS MY SONG!"

It was on this program on 91X—the Top 9 at 9. People had to call in and name all nine songs that were played starting at 9:00. So people were calling in and they would say, "Number three was Pearl Jam, and number two was Tori Amos, and number one was Nirvana."

And the DJ would say, "NO. WRONG."

And the next person would guess that her song was Sarah McLachlan. No one got it. And Jewel loved it. She was laughing because no one knew who she was.

What Jewel single set a record for longevity on *Billboard's* "Hot 100"?

"You Were Meant For Me"

Alan   In 1995, the album had just been released and was going nowhere. Jewel was doing what's called a residency tour. It worked

What were your three worst gigs?

1 Playing on top of a van for passersby in the middle of Times Square.
2 Singing for the grand opening of a shoe store.
3 Playing at a high school in Detroit at 9 A.M. for a bunch of kids who thought they were going to see "Jewell" perform (a girl rap act out at the time). Needless to say, they were very disappointed when a folk chick walked out.

13

really well for her. They would rotate the same venues each day of the week for a month.

Lenedra At the time, radio simply would not play her, so our challenge was to integrate this folk-pop singer into the grunge world. We knew that building a fan base was the route to take. We did that by sending her on figure-eight tours, where she would rotate through a series of cities on a weekly loop. She did San Diego, Chico, Portland and Seattle. She would hit the same place in each city every week, and the crowd would grow from just a handful of people to standing room only by the end of the month.

Pre-show, This Way Tour, Vienna, VA, 6/19/02

Bibi I went a couple of times when she was just touring in the van. I went out just to visit her when she was doing one of those residency tours. I just flew out and met her in Connecticut once and traveled down to Washington, D.C., with her. At point it was just her friend Jerry, the doorman from the InnerChange, who was driving her around.

14

Alan Once she got out of California, there was quite a distance between the cities. So it was literally do the gig, then drive all night to the next gig. They just had a rental car. Just Jewel and a friend traveling together.

Monty Jewel went out on the road with a friend of hers who was kind of acting as the tour manager, driving her around. But because of the emphasis on promoting Jewel, rather than just going out there and doing a concert tour, she was often traveling on her own. They would put her on a plane somewhere, and the guy who was driving would be left to catch up by road. Sometimes she'd be picked up at the airport by a radio rep from Atlantic, taken to a radio station and then dropped at a hotel, and then she'd be sitting around there waiting for this guy to pick her up and take her across to the sound check.

> **With which country legend has Jewel recorded two duets?**
>
> Merle Haggard

Bibi I think at the time her album had been released and still no one was listening to her. She was playing in these coffeehouses on the East Coast, driving through snowstorms. She would show up, and there would be like three people there drinking beers. She would get up there with her purple polyester pants and her vinyl jacket and her little pigtails and play for like half an hour, forty minutes. And she would play like there were a thousand people there.

A lot of times I was sitting there thinking, "Oh God." I felt so bad for her because no one was listening. She was selling out Spreckels Theatre in San Diego, which has about 1,500 seats, so she had achieved some level of success, and she was used to playing larger venues at that point. And, plus, she was playing all kinds of places when she was growing up. She would just be like it was something she had to do. I think she knew that she was paying her dues.

seeing SPIKES all over

Alan The first year the album went nowhere. A year after *Pieces of You* was released, it hadn't gone gold.

Shane There was this resistance. A lot of radio stations said, "We will not play a young girl folk artist with a guitar." She was a bit different. She was coming in at a peak time when man was king on the radio. Nirvana and things like that.

Lenedra This was 1995. Jewel was basically a quasi-folk-rock-pop chick in a very hip-hop/grunge world. And with the release of this latest album it was somewhat the same. Jewel doesn't fit perfectly into today's musical environment either, where pop is really predominant. So the challenge for us is to find ways to integrate her into that landscape. Going directly to the fans is what works for us. They don't think in terms of musical categories, as radio and industry people do.

This Way Tour, Fort Lauderdale, FL, 6/15/02

Monty KROQ had this thing they do with artists. They'll play a track like in the early hours of the morning. And they gauge the response to it. If they get a favorable response, they'll put it on the play list. They'll give it some low spins, and if they continue to get a good response, they'll build it up. For some rea-

This Way Tour, Fort Lauderdale, FL, 6/15/02

son they decided to play "Who Will Save Your Soul" in the wee small hours, and they started to get a favorable response for it. I think it was in the same week, the last few weeks towards the end of that tour, Atlantic, buoyed by the support of KROQ, decided to stop pushing "You Were Meant for Me" and go back to "Who Will Save Your Soul."

Around the same time, VH1 decided to start giving some good exposure to the video for "Who Will Save Your Soul." Suddenly both things started happening again, the video and the radio picking up interest at the same time.

Plans changed completely. Instead of coming off the road and going into the studio to record another album, they were seeing sales spikes and radio spikes all over the country. So a year after its release and relentless touring, people were catching on to Jewel.

Jewel's hard work, going around doing these shows and going off and doing radio interviews everywhere and sitting on the radio playing a few songs, was starting to pay off. Spins were increasing, sales were starting to pick up.

So they decided to book her into a club tour, headlining. She went out on the road with a band—a little band was put together, about three or four players. During the course of that tour, which was about three weeks in May, *Pieces of You* went gold. "Who Will Save Your Soul" was a big hit. The record just kept going.

Michael   In 1996, when *Pieces of You* had sold about 50,000 copies, I basically called people from all the different studios. I called producers, casting directors, directors, movie stars, and invited them to this show of hers. Usually, when you invite people to those things, you know, you invite 200 and you expect about 25. But for this one I got about 80 percent attendance. And no one really knew who she was, but everybody sort of knew they *should* know her. They just didn't know why yet.

I remember the head of Universal Pictures calling me after that and saying, "I'm going to remember that show for 25 years." People just knew something was happening. They could feel it.

Alan   Within two months of going gold, *Pieces of You* went platinum. By Christmas, it was double platinum.

Jewel's rise to the top was at such a rapid pace, once things finally got rolling, that she had to constantly make small adjustments to herself in order to preserve her inner core. At the same time she had to try to convince herself that it was all really happening. Try to imagine suddenly going from being a very private, sensitive, even somewhat introverted person in love with poetry and music to someone the whole world suddenly wants to know. Your first reaction would probably be to put up your defenses and wait for the blow to come—the flood of criticism unleashed by those who think you're an imposter.

And then, if still nothing happened, you would probably be in such shock and disbelief that you would hesitate to step forward and accept this new position. Having never spent any time in your past making a plan or devising a way to be in such a position, you would probably feel unprepared for the job and overwhelmed with the thought of the challenge.

Jewel never really planned on being a musician. She was just tired of working jobs that led to nowhere, while barely making enough money to get by. She had started putting her writing to music, and as her chords married her lyrics, the outcome was a collection of totally unique songs, full of her emotion and carried by her voice. Still, she never really thought her music was better than anyone else's. Or that it was all that great—she just knew it was honest. So when she signed with Atlantic Records, it came as a great surprise to see her first album eventually do so well. When it finally hit, Jewel's career took off overnight, and rather than be crushed by all the challenges that brought, she took the proverbial bull by the horns. That's something I truly admire about her—finding the courage to live up to her dreams.

And so life goes on and the challenges, and rewards, keep coming. This chapter covers the good and bad, the ups and downs, that Jewel has encountered as a famous person. But in the end, you'll see that the good—not the money, not the power, not perks, but the fact that Jewel can continue to create art and help others—outweighs the downside of things, and she just keeps going.

Atz Lee Kilcher

What are your guilty pleasures?

I love lingerie and jewelry. And I don't know if I should say this, but I like firearms. Ty just gave me a lever action Winchester 30-30. It's pretty much a vintage gun—the gun that won the West. They made a limited series of 500 with Ty, to honor his breaking the record with seven all-around titles. It's beautiful. I have number two.

Lee Of course she's changed. Everyone should change. It would be just terrible if she didn't. She has grown—matured, learned so much. So she's changed in positive ways. But I've seen other people who became famous and it's like, "Wow. What a shame. What's happened to that person?" She's not one of those stories.

Monty At the end of the day, she's still pretty much the same down-to-earth person that she always was—that person who grew up in Alaska. And you can see all the influences that her mom's had on her and, in some respects, that her dad's had. She's still essentially that same person, though obviously her experiences are going to have an effect on her.

West What *has* changed over the years isn't so much her, but how others perceive her. They now see her as a famous person, and they are in awe of that or are now intimidated by her. It's a little awkward for them. But she hasn't changed. It's a really funny dynamic.

Lee She isn't trying to jump in on celebrity circles. She doesn't like a lot of bull. She can only put up with so much superficial crap before she really has to walk away.

Michael She's confident of herself and knows who she is, so she's comfortable in any situation. But is that her world? No, not necessarily. But she's

Who gave Jewel a miniature silver suitcase as a gift for opening her show?

Melissa Etheridge

unbelievable in any circumstances. I've seen her talk to the biggest stars in the world. I've seen her talk to the heads of major corporations, to Tom Cruise, Bob Dylan. You name it.

T-Bone   I've learned that she does diva as a joke, because it's just so silly to her. And sometimes people won't understand that it's a joke. You have to know her.

Monty   Anyone that travels on business the way Jewel does—so extensively—they're going to want to stay in nicer hotels and they want to have five-hour flights on private jets or first class because of the amount of times you do it, and how wearing it gets.

But she flies coach when she'd rather get going than wait for a seat, and she never travels with an entourage. She hates large groups.

Stephen   She doesn't like limos. Often it's easier to travel in one, because of the privacy and space and to get her from place to place. But she'd rather get out and walk around the corner into a meeting, rather than make a scene by getting out of a limo.

some COOl PERKS

Shane   There are some cool perks to being a celebrity, and you'd be crazy not to take advantage of them. These great opportunities and encounters started happening more and more as her fame started to grow.

Bibi   We were on this island—Daydream Island in Australia—for four or five days where she had to play like three songs. One night she gets up there, plays her songs, and the rest of the time we rented a little boat and went across to another island. We just relaxed. We went snorkeling; we sat in the sun. It was just such a scam. She kept calling it that: "This is the biggest scam of the century!" Having the record company pay for her to go to

Any examples of when you were spoofing diva and people didn't get it?

When I was filming the Ang Lee movie, people seemed awkward around me because I wasn't an actor, I was a pop star! So I thought the best icebreaker would be to make fun of the whole diva thing. But I forgot that my humor can be very dry and people didn't always know I was kidding.

Like, I walked into the catering area and dramatically swooped my arms and said, very melodramatically, "Everybody out!" And the room just cleared. There wasn't even anyone left to tell it was just a joke. They actually took me seriously. I couldn't believe it.

Australia with her boyfriend and her best friend, so they can sit in the sun after playing a concert for fifteen minutes.

This Way Tour, Toronto, ONT, 6/28/02

Shane   We had a kind of cool experience going through the Rock and Roll Hall of Fame. They closed the place up and opened it late for us. And we all went through there all on our own. Halfway through the tour they started playing her music through the loudspeakers. So we were wandering through the Hall of Fame, and Jewel was the guide. I can't remember a damn thing she said, but it was pretty cool. She's like, "Oh yeah! This is Hendrix's guitar!" She was just hyper, running around the place.

Lenedra   She started noticing how she was being noticed, and how that opened some doors. People she really admired were suddenly introducing themselves to her. When Jewel met Bob Dylan, he had actually watched her set, then came down into her dressing room after the show. And he said, "Yeah, that song you were doing . . ." and he recited a bunch of lyrics. She said, "Oh, that's 'Sometimes It Be That Way'!"

He said, "That's really good storytelling. That's a really good song."

She really enjoyed that he had not only watched her set but that he had remembered the lyrics to one of her songs. They talked songwriting, and it was one of her first experiences with having an in-depth conversation about music with one of her peers. That meant a lot to her.

double**TAKE**

Monty She's not a glamorous-looking person when she's offstage. She can put on a hat and a pair of sunglasses and tie her hair up and off she goes. She can go shopping or wandering off somewhere and nobody will notice her.

Mark She can just go and do whatever. That really surprised me when I first met her. She'd just go hang out. I guess she kind of blends in.

Brady I remember one time we were in Paris, and I think that we went out shopping. I was with my girlfriend and Jewel, and we went shopping around a little bit. So anyway we went back to the gig, and Jewel didn't have her laminate [backstage pass]. Well hell, she don't need no laminate! It was her damn show. I never will forget it. This lady at the door was busting her balls! I'm like, "Look, this really is her!" Jewel stayed cool the whole time because she didn't want to go there. I thought that was pretty cool, 'cause I would have been like, "Bitch, look, let me in this mo—." But she just joked about it. She said, "If I tell you I'm a groupie and sleeping with the band, will you let me in?"

Shane She's always pretty conscious about people knowing who she is. It's not like it's a big deal to her, but you can see a moment when people realize it.

Rumor has it that a few hardcore Jewel fans in Japan have done what in order to look like Jewel?

Had their teeth surgically altered to look like Jewel's

Bibi Most people will do a double take, and you'll see them out of the corner of your eye go, "Oh my God! It's Jewel!" But most people, if she does have to engage with them, they'll say to her, "Do people tell you that you look like Jewel?" And she'll say, "Yeah." And leave it at that.

This Way Tour, Vienna, VA, 6/19/02

Doug   We were in Florida, West Palm Beach, doing the Spirit Tour in '99, and she had rung me up in the morning and said, "Let's go surfing." We were right on the beach there at the Ritz, I think. So I went out with my nice robe and my surf trunks and my John Deere hat, and looked at the surf. It looked pretty good.

So we went up to this kid, and I asked him if he knew of any surfboard rental places. And he said, "Yeah, there's one about two miles down the beach."

I took him aside and said, "Do you like Jewel?"

He said, "Yeah, I love her."

Jewel was right there, just out of earshot, staring at the surf, but he hadn't recognized her.

I said, "This is Jewel. We want to go surfing. Do you know anyone we could just borrow some surfboards from?"

And he just handed me his board, and he ran down the beach to get his brother's board. It was great, great surfing because a hurricane was coming in. He sacrificed a great day of surfing. He came back with his brother's board, and we were out there for like two hours, Jewel and I.

We got him and his friend tickets to the show that night. We got him backstage, the whole deal.

Is sense of humor something you look for in a guy?

Sense of humor—I never really thought about it. Self-awareness I'd say counts more than anything. To know where you are at any given time is difficult, male or female. You get people acting out and not quite knowing why—all that's very unattractive.

This Way Tour, Interlochen, MI, 7/5/02

Stephen People are very gracious most of the time. But they can be quite pushy. Human nature is such that people go after what they want and they don't always consider someone else's space or someone's mind frame. Like if Jewel's out with friends having a quiet time, for the most part they're gracious, but sometimes they'll just plow in and interrupt her and things like that. It goes with the territory.

Anybody that gets in the media eye, like her, anybody with any normal way of thinking, is going to have to get a little bit guarded. The media can only write about how great you are for so long. Then they have to start finding other angles. I think a lot of the time writers will try to muster up anything they can to tell a story. It's hard to explain. You have to realize that you're dealing with all kinds of people in the media—from those that love you to those that are jealous of you to people that can't wait for you to be a bitch. I think that can make you really guarded. If everyone were honest and had good intentions, I think that being in the public eye so much would be a lot easier. I think that's only in a perfect world.

Your life has to have some privacy. Everyone else's life does. I'm talking about your everyday Joe U.S.A. They have their privacy. But they can decide when they're private and when they're not. Sometimes when you're in the public eye like she is, you have other people choosing for you what's private and what's not. Really nothing's private. You have to become guarded in ways, just to look after yourself. She's definitely able to take care of herself.

I think she's hard to get to know. Whenever you become a celebrity, like she is, it's real easy to have friends. People will want to be your friend from the very first time they meet you. That's a weird thing. I think she's the type of person that wants to earn people's friendship and vice versa. She wants them to earn hers. Whenever you're a celebrity, you'll find that people will laugh at anything you say and think you're smart no matter what you do. And they're always there to pat you on the back and be your yes-man. That's a real false sense of security or friendship. I think she's smart enough to see past that. She wants to get to know people really well and for the friendship to be earned, and I think that's a good quality.

Your life has to have some PRIVACY.

Ty Murray

Bibi Sometimes people give her a hard time just because she's famous. Like this one time, she sang the national anthem at this rodeo. Then when she came back to sit down, she put on a sweatshirt with a hood. So some guy was saying, really sarcastically, "OH, WHERE'S JEWEL? I DON'T KNOW WHERE JEWEL IS. CAN'T SEE HER, SHE'S IN DISGUISE."

I wanted to throw something at him.

Shane One time, she tried to upgrade to first class. We're standing at the counter, facing this lady who's saying, "Well, it's pretty full."

And Jewel's like, "Oh, could you please just check?"

"Well, give me your passport."

And she looks at the passport and she looks at Jewel and her face gets stern. And, you know, you saw the light go on. And then you see her face get set, and she goes, "It's full," without even bothering to really check.

meet & GREET

Monty She often seems more comfortable on a stage with her guitar, in front of 1,500 people or 5,000, than she does in a room with 15 people at a meet-and-greet.

Brandon I remember her going to one of the meet-and-greets, and these girls were just freaking out. They had the signs, the T-shirts, the whole bit. And they were just freaking out, jumping up and down, crying, hugging her. I think she copes with it pretty well, but it must get hard. Fans like that are awfully delicate; they're very observant of every little thing you do and can often misconstrue things, depending on your response to them.

Mark They all seem to know the music better than we do. They sing every lyric. They seem really loyal and totally into the music. It's cool to watch it. I'm sure she has her crazy fans, too, but most are just dying to watch her sing and sing along with her.

Alan Sometimes fans wait outside a venue hoping she's going to come out and sign autographs and things like that, and they get really upset if she doesn't. A lot of times she either doesn't know they're out there or she's just not into doing it. I think she's honest with them, and herself, about that kind of thing. She does do a lot of selfless things like that, but I think she's just really honest about how she's feeling at any given time.

Not counting her famous VW van (which is in storage), how many cars does Jewel own?

One—
a Jeep Cherokee

It's impossible to be everything to everybody all the time. Sometimes the day of work and the show exhaust her to the point that there's nothing left to give.

this grace, this touch

Stephen   Quite often she'll bring backstage some child whose dream it was to meet her—some have been kids with serious illnesses, on the brink of death. It's so beautiful to watch that moment, when she can touch someone's soul. I'm blessed to be a part of it.

This Way Tour, Interlochen, MI, 7/5/02

This Way Tour, Pittsburgh, PA, 6/29/02

Monty   When we were out doing *Spirit*, we got a request from a radio station in
        Minneapolis. This lady had been trying in some way to make contact with
        Jewel. She ended up doing it through this radio station. She had a son who
        was really ill. He was in a wheelchair; his sight was slowly starting to fail.
        Something was really taking a toll on him. His mum said, "It would be really
        great, it would really lift his spirits, if there was any way he could meet
        Jewel."
            And Jewel said, "Let's arrange to meet him." This would be before the
        show. This kid came back in his wheelchair with his mum and one or two of
        the radio people. And there was hardly a dry eye in the area. It was effortless
        for her. Some people have this grace, this touch. Everyone who was there
        was practically in tears over how genuinely tender this moment was. She

was genuinely connecting with this lad, who couldn't speak, but just the look on his face—you could see how much it meant to him.

She was either stroking his head or his hand, holding his hand, talking to him. It was amazing. One of the most incredible human interactions I've seen in a situation like that.

This Way Tour, Toronto, ONT, 6/28/02

Sharon   He was just the sweetest boy. What I watch her do is, there's nobody else in the room but her and the child—everybody else fades away. Even though the room is full, she is so focused that it's like she's just there with that child. There's just like this tunnel between the two of them.

After meeting him—he gave her gifts and she gave him gifts, signed a book for him, a T-shirt—she calls together four or five of us on the staff, and we circle up and hold hands and she says a prayer for that little boy.

Then she goes out and performs for him—performs a song just for him—and it seems that the crowd has just, once again, faded away.

she **can't** act normal

Shane One thing really illustrates how she can't act normal anymore. You know, you're allowed to once in a while just cuss somebody out, or go through a little road rage here and there. And people just understand that it's an isolated occurrence. But, you know, when you're a celebrity, you call somebody a name once and it gets in a tabloid and that's your label, you know? You have to be gracious all the time. You lose your ability to interact with people normally.

So we're in this store, buying boots and Western apparel. We're there looking around, and this girl's like looking at us a little bit. After a while, it's obvious that she's spotted her and she's trying to work up the nerve, or trying to settle an issue. She's been nice a couple of times, pointed out an item or two. But she's like starting to brim over.

And she says, "Does anyone ever tell you that you look just like Jewel?"

Jewel goes, "Yeah. I get that a lot. I am Jewel."

The girl's all, "Nah."

So Jewel's like, "Okay. Whatever."

And so we're walking around, looking at some stuff, and the girl comes back up to us again. Jewel's saying things to her like, "Do you have this in a different size?"

The girl wouldn't even answer the question. She's like, "You're not really Jewel."

"Yeah. I am."

It got to the point where she wouldn't leave us alone. She just wouldn't believe us. She brought it up, saying, "Aren't you Jewel?"

What's something you've learned about the biz that will help those coming up?

There are two ways to go about a career. One is the pursuit of art; one is pursuing celebrity. Some people pursuing celebrity use art as a vehicle. But it's only a vehicle. And if you're pursuing art, celebrity's a side effect, possibly—if you click with the culture. That's a really conscious decision that I think every artist should make from the get-go. And base every career decision over the years on that decision. Because it will either support art or support celebrity.

31

And Jewel kept saying, "Look, I'm Jewel."

The girl goes away and then comes back, saying, "I just can't believe it. I love all your music. Are you pulling my leg? Are you really Jewel?"

Jewel's like, "Lady, I'm Jewel."

She says, "Let me see your license to prove it."

So Jewel's like, "I CAN'T BELIEVE IT. Come on. Could you give me a little space?"

So for like a half an hour, it was, "Are you really Jewel?" Like from across the store. She just wouldn't leave us alone. And Jewel was getting really upset. She had been talking to me in the car on the way there about how her life has changed: It's hard for her to go out, go shopping, interact with family if we want to go do something. We don't get together that often. So finally Jewel's like, "Look, just leave me alone. I'm shopping with my brother. I don't care if you believe that I'm Jewel or not, just leave me alone."

We go to pay, and of course, she's paying with her credit card and shows her ID. It's a guy who rings us up and we leave the store. And the girl comes running out after us and says, "I just want you to know that I don't care who you are, you just can't treat normal people like that."

Do you and your mom ever argue?

No, not really. We're both pretty rational people. We're both pretty willful, so it's not as though we don't have disagreements. One of us is usually right. Or we disagree and don't do it. When it comes to career decisions, there's nothing ever that's so unclear that we'd actually disagree. There's usually one right way to go about things.

who is this funny-looking, snaggly-tooth, little folk-pop music chick ⎯⎯ANYWAY?

Atz Lee She takes a lot of hits in the media, and it's not so much that it doesn't hurt but it's more that just sitting around crying about it doesn't do much.

Shane Both my mom and dad would mention to us as kids that, you know, a critic in the newspaper was really harsh on us. But they were never really personally affected by it. I think there were a couple of times I kind of saw that maybe they thought it was going to affect their career or the show. But, you know, it really became obvious watching that it's all just a cycle. You get some good reviews, you get some bad reviews. It's not always anything personal. Everyone's got different tastes. As a kid, getting to see the process was really valuable.

I think she's doing fine. I don't think fame has had any negative effects on her. She's the same with me as she has always been. And with other people, too. I see her with her band, her crew, the people around her on tour, and she's great with everyone. She's always ready to put her arm around someone, to say thanks and treat others very humbly.

I performed with Jewel in three shows last summer, and she still has elements in her approach that were there in the beginning. What I really love is her style of talking and storytelling when performing, maybe because it reminds me of myself. Talking about her songs and how they came to be. Telling the audience about herself—that's part of the whole package.

That's something that has always amazed me—how she's been able to read the audience and get a strong response. I saw that right from the start. I was once at a concert with her back east during the Tiny Lights Tour. The crowd was rowdy and she wanted to sing a quiet song. So she just stood at the mic and said, "Shhh. Shhh." Just shushing them like a mama shushes a baby. I was backstage and part of me was just terrified. I thought, "You know, Jewel, there's like 500,000 college kids out there. They've been drinking and they're rowdy, and you're up there onstage telling them, 'Shush.'"

But another part of me just felt extremely proud. And the crowd just got quieter and quieter. Finally, it was totally still and she started singing this beautiful, quiet song that she wanted a certain atmosphere for. It brought tears to my eyes seeing how my little girl found a way to get what she wanted so she could perform that song. She'll just use whatever—sometimes being quiet or using humor to get what she needs for the song. You see something like that and you know that she has what it takes, that she's going to be fine.

And the crowd just got quieter and quieter.

Atz Kilcher

Alan   A lot of the bashing comes from journalists and interviewers who have really done no homework about her. A lot of her fan base gets really frustrated by that, and they're always defending her. It's a really interesting thing. I think it's like an easy way out—to bash her; it takes less thought.

Monty   Part of the problem is being so young and getting compared, like Jewel sometimes does, to people like Joni Mitchell. But everyone's perception of Joni Mitchell is generally Joni Mitchell now, like Bob Dylan. They've been around, doing what they do, for 30 years, and it's not a fair comparison to make.

Are shows like the concert in Bearsville your favorite way to give something back to your fans?

I don't really see doing shows like the one in Bearsville as "giving back" to the fans. It's mutual. I get a lot from it. I enjoy it. I'm happiest alone onstage with a small crowd that I can visit with and feel as much as they feel me. I do have to say my fans make it easy. They're very cool people.

I did another one of those free shows in Nashville in 2001. Afterwards, I left the venue with Ty, and there were all these fans that had driven across the country to see me just quietly waiting for me to cross in front of them to get to my car. They thanked me for the show and away we drove.

continued on page 35

Shane Sometimes you can't help but take it personally. If the critics say they don't like the music, that's one thing. Half the time, it's more like, "Who is this funny-looking, snaggly-tooth, little folk-pop music chick anyway?" And then it gets personal.

Alan It's an act of conscious dissent—not to get trapped in that cynical, negative attitude all the time. I grew up in the '70s and '80s, and I saw that develop.

Shane I think it is obvious that if you look at her lyrics and look at her poetry, there are a lot of street smarts there.

Alan It was so refreshing to see somebody that was so anticynical and who was not at all apologetic about it.

Which title was bestowed on Jewel by the American Music Awards in 1997?

Best New Artist

Shane Isn't that funny how being an optimist can really bring out the pessimist in somebody else? You want to test it: It's almost like a faith issue. If somebody's apparently optimistic, some part of you wants to test it. To see if it's real. I think so much of her presentation is kind of down-home, like a real person. Then you get this optimism streak and it's like, "Whoa, is she putting up a front here?"

Atz Lee It's something you take on with the position of being a rock star. She didn't really know that was part of it because she didn't set out to be a rock star. So that made it hard because when it did start happening, she couldn't make a decision right there because it was already in forward motion. You can't exactly jump off at that point. She really wanted to carry on with her music, and part of those things that went along with it was all this media craziness on the side.

Shane   She's pretty resilient. She can take the hits and roll with the punches and just keep on going.

something
that RINGS TRUE

continued from page 34

Sharon   Jewel comes from her own heart. She has an authenticity to her. I think that authenticity that comes out—through her music and through her poetry—is what touches the hearts of people, especially young people. Young people come in and they're looking for something that rings true. And when Jewel sings, she goes in and it's like she touches a spark inside them.

Stuart   She communicates and they get where she's coming from, and I think that's the most important thing. She's just honest and believable.

Michael   I used to call her my secret weapon. Because I knew I could send her into a meeting and I knew she would come out of that meeting with that person falling in love with her, basically, and wanting to find a way to work with her. When people really get a chance to know her— which were the situations I'd try to set up in meetings with directors—they really under-

Ty was freaked out. He had never seen anything like that before. He's used to the usual pushy and frantic crush from fans. I really enjoy that my fans understand what I do enough to respect me for my talent and who I am. The respect is mutual.

Which one of Jewel's music videos appears to be set primarily in a women's bathroom?

"Who Will Save Your Soul"

stand who she is and what she does in just a few moments. She's so genuine. They see it.

A good example is when I introduced to her to Steven Spielberg. Steven's meetings are usually 15 minutes, but she spent an hour and a half in there. I remember she happened to have her guitar with her because she was going to rehearsal right afterwards, but she didn't bring it in the room. So she went to the car and got the guitar and played him a song. He asked her if he could write down the words, and I remember he folded the paper up and put it in his breast pocket and said, "I'm going to keep them right next to my heart."

Lenedra   The comment that people make most frequently, whether they're her peers, her fans or leaders in the industry, is a recognition of her authenticity, her down-to-earth quality. Her realness, if you will. And what people are often surprised about is her sense of humor.

Pre-show, This Way Tour, Atlanta, GA, 6/17/02

West   Her fans sense that she's pretty accessible and familiar. It seems like the greatest desires, in terms of pictures and video requests, are shots of her living everyday life. They like to see her interact in the same world they live in. I think that's what they find appealing.

Sharon   It's not that they're loyal to the music. I think they're loyal to Jewel. No matter what she chooses to do, she'll still have support. She'll still have the fans there. It goes beyond what she presents. It's all about who she is and how she presents it.

> **Jewel played at the Inaugural Ball for which president?**
>
> Bill Clinton

Alan   There was a girl, Duff, from Kansas, who one day posted the question to the EDA list, "Wouldn't it be nice if Jewel did a private concert for the EDAs?" [The EveryDay Angels (EDAs) were the first online Jewel discussion group, who, among other things, formed their own humanitarian foundation.] And it just happened to be perfect timing, because Jewel and Lenedra were in Bearsville working on the follow-up to *Pieces of You*, doing studio sessions there. She had been rehearsing in the Bearsville Theatre, which is a really cool place that Albert Grossman built for Bob Dylan and the Band in the '60s. It's basically a barn with a cozy intimate theater and a great PA system permanently installed. It seats about 300 people.

So anyway, Lenedra got that EDA message, and she and Jewel discussed it. The timing was perfect and they agreed that Jewel would like to do a show for the EDAs as long as they would come to Bearsville and make the arrangements.

What ended up happening is that people from all over North America that had been on this mailing list all converged and met for the first time. It took everyone from being just anonymous names on a mailing list to being real people. Everybody hung out for three days. They camped together. And everybody that attended this event left significantly changed—and just amazed at Jewel and Lenedra's generosity. Not to mention that those two shows were, at that time, the two best performances she had ever done, in my opinion.

One of the reasons was because it was the perfect audience. You could

"Phyllis Barnabee" refers to what Jewel promo single?

"You Were Meant For Me"

hear a pin drop the whole time she was playing. Those nights she played for a solid four hours, and she didn't play anything off the album.

With the EDAs, I think a lot of their loyalty is a result of that "Jewelstock" experience. I think everyone was amazed that all these people, including Jewel and Lenedra, could get together and pull off such a monumental event with no monetary concerns. There was no cover charge for the show; it was strictly just an experience they were looking to have. The media never knew about it and Jewel never said anything about it to the media. That just blew a lot of people away. That they were more concerned with giving something back to the fans and bringing all these people together than any kind of monetary concerns really took a lot of people by surprise. It's just not the way a lot of the music industry works anymore. That was the turning point for a lot of really loyal fans—fans that are still there to this day.

Sharon   She gives them the courage and the hope, by looking at a young girl who lived on the beach and lived in a car, that you can have your dreams. And in that, you can help other people fulfill their dreams. That's what her fans are doing.

For an artist it all comes down to the creative moment, that creative process. That's their job, after all: to create. And the outcome of that process is truly the deciding factor in regards to what makes a musician popular. Are they able to reach people through their music? Can they create a song that carries in it their character, their emotions, in ways that people feel moved, touched, comforted? This is a challenge, considering that there are only so many chord patterns and melodies out there. Yet, it happens in Jewel's songs. How it all comes together is largely a mystery to the listener, who only hears the final product. This chapter tries to shed some light on Jewel's unique approach to making music.

In many cases, if you ask the musician about their creative process, they stare back at you with a puzzled face, and after a brief pause they finally state that they are at times so focused on creating the song that they don't really keep tabs on how they do it. The process of creation is often a mystery to those doing the creating. With Jewel, this process is constant and ongoing. It's not something she does sitting at a desk somewhere. She's doing it all the time, whether she's observing the stories going on around her, thinking about what it is she wants to say, or actually sitting down with a guitar and pencil.

I think photographer and old friend West puts it best when he states, "The most authentic Jewel is when she's in the creative mode." Comfort comes in wide ranges as far as musicians go. Some are most comfortable performing songs that have been rehearsed and rerehearsed and have a known response, while other musicians, such as Jewel, find themselves most relaxed when they're creating something on the spot. That's when she's fully alive. Sometimes this happens onstage; sometimes among friends, family, but most often when she's alone. Whatever the circumstances, Jewel is most at one with herself when she is in the process of making art.

Atz Lee Kilcher

A universe in her HEAD

West The most authentic Jewel is when she's in the creative mode. The one thing I find fascinating about her creative process is the many ways it manifests. Not just in music but in her writing and her painting and everything she does.

I saw her at the Beacon Theater in New York about five or six years ago. I think she was touring the first album. And I remember people standing up and giving her ovations after verses of songs. I had never seen that before. I was kind of blown away by that. It shows how much they were connecting with her lyrics.

She's a real true-blue poet. The thing that makes her a special artist is her lyrics. She has completely solid point-of-view, and her poetic voice is completely intact. That's driving the whole thing; that's driving Jewel's songs: her lyrics. She just writes what she writes. All her songs speak to you. When she came over, when I knew I was going to write with her, I already knew how good she was. She sat down and played like about 12 songs, and every song had a message and every song had a style to it and the lyrics were all great.

The voice doesn't mean anything unless your lyrics are touching people.

She has the vocal technique. Jewel is a proper singer's singer. But her voice has character. Jewel's a

She's a real TRUE-BLUE poet.

great writer, great singer, great instrumentalist. All the big ones who sort of make history do that. She comes out of that tradition. She's a great contemporary voice coming out of that singer-writer-instrumentalist tradition. She came out of doing her songs as an acoustic artist, but I don't think of her as a folk artist. I think of her as a songwriter—a contemporary poetic voice. But having said that, growing up in Alaska, she grew up on all the folk music and all the country music, so she's a real, honest proponent of that kind of music. She could be a country singer, and she's a legitimate singer of folk music.

I think Jewel's the real deal. All artists that are the real deal are much needed. Those are the ones that matter in the long span of history. She's a legitimate singer-songwriter, and she has something to say and she touches people and speaks to people. That's a real powerful thing. And it's a positive thing that she does touch people because what she has to say is good.

Rick Nowels

Shane She loves photography and drawing and painting, singing—everything from show tunes to opera.

Sharon It still boils down to music. It's under everything really. When you paint, there's music to it. When you write, music feeds the words. For her, I think music is what it all comes down to—her music, her voice.

Recording Session, Los Angeles, CA, 3/27/01

Brandon She loves to write. I remember we'd be sitting in the airport, and she'd be writing some ditty about the potbellied guy across the aisle. Writing songs, poems, journal entries.

Monty There were times during the tours promoting *Pieces of You* where we were just checked in at an airport and she had her guitar slung over her shoulder, and she'd go off into the corner. She'd get the guitar out, and pencil and notepad, and she had this idea in her head and she'd sit there and sing it to herself. And she'd write the lyrics down. And she'd keep doing it to keep remembering the song, so she didn't forget it. And she'd have this little bit floating around in her head, until she got the time to work on it enough that she didn't forget it. Or she got the chance to sing it into a tape recorder.

Do you think we live in a special era for humanity?

When you look at what's at our disposal, in terms of science and spirituality, it's a really exciting time. We have more science, more technology, more schooling at our disposal. Just a bit of apathy. I'd like to see more intellectual communities forming, like in the past, where the arts and the sciences got together. I think we suffer for that. But I do think we'll see more inventions and discoveries in coming years than ever before.

Recording Studio, Nashville, TN, 7/11/01

Sharon   She started writing as a very young child, partly because I think that was her best friend. It was a place where she could be totally honest and put down who she was, then see it reflected back to her in the words. It was like a mirror. She could see, authentically, who she was on paper. And then she would see what she wanted to change or grow into.

What historical era especially fascinates you?

I really like history. It's not a topic I enjoyed in school, but for some reason I've become really drawn to it. I can't think of a period in history that I'm not fascinated by. And I especially like seeing what vices directly correlated to the religious feel of the time. You know, whatever was banned by religion or God or social circumstances resulted in strong pockets of deviance. That really interests me.

Recording Studio, Nashville, TN, 7/11/01

Stephen   I'll find little—little!—pieces of paper with drawings on them, ideas for a song, ideas for poetry. And I don't even think she calculates what they're for. It just kind of flows out of her. She's not like, "I need a song about this or this." It's more about, "Whatever it turns into, it turns into." And it could be nothing. Most of it gets scattered or lost. I'll come across them and try to collect them, or she'll hand me a wad of crumpled notes and say, "Hang on to these." And then she might never ask me for them. It all goes in her head.

There's no real structure when we write. Usually, I'll start playing guitar and singing a song and she'll start singing. She'll understand exactly where I'm going with it. Like, I may come up with a melody, some words, and then we just kind of both scat sing words and melodies back to each other, and we're not afraid to say, "No, I don't like that. What about this word?"

A lot of times what I say will be over the top. And she'll say, "No. You can't say that." And then we'll argue. "Why not?"

For instance, like in "You Were Meant For Me," I really wanted to say, "I'm half alive but I feel mostly dead." She didn't like that, because, I think she thought it was depressing. I said, "Well, I'll accept `I break the yolks and make a smiley face' if you accept this one." It's a trade-off, which is cool. Nobody has a defined thing that they do. There are no set duties. It's both people throwing in ideas. Strange ideas. Lyrics. Melodies. Which is cool. I like it like that, because you can end up with whatever you want, or be whoever you want to be in the song. I don't like it if something's really defined. We're both songwriters; we both have a sense of what we like.

She'll definitely take a song that I would make that would have an edge to it and she'll make it prettier. She's good at that.

It's a TRADE-OFF, WHICH IS COOl.

Steve Poltz

Lee She has a great holographic universe in her head. I've always looked at her mind as if she has it filled with files. And she has them categorized. She takes other files when it applies and gets more information by combining two of them together. And it's kind of how she writes a song. A lot of people wonder, "What inspired her to write this one song?" But actually, the song might come from five totally separate elements.

She'll call her message machine and leave what she starts on it. She'll start working on a song; she'll play what she has. And I learned, after seeing this happen, not to count on the original movement to remain that way. It's like all the elements are already there, but she just has to piece them together.

busting OUT
playing

Alan   In general, whenever she wrote things, she would just perform them that day. She would often invite fans up from the audience to hold up the lyrics for her because she hadn't even memorized them yet. She's really gutsy in that way. I admire that about her—that she's really willing to go out there and try a new song on an audience. And I think that's one of the things that makes her so fascinating to see live. You never really know what she may end up playing on any given night.

Doug   She would come in with an idea like at sound check. She wrote the songs. And as far as arrangements go, she would pretty much have the arrangements already done.

Trey   She knows inherently what's going to make a song better, and it's all in her head. She's like a great composer. They know, before they put it on paper, how it's going to sound. And that's what separates the great songwriters from everyone else, I think.

Brady   She'll just come busting out playing, or she'll try something new or write something and play it at a gig. That's always hip 'cause, you know, the show never gets boring that way. It's like, "I got a new song." We do it at sound check, run over it and then do it on the gig that night.

Alan   There are some amazing things she's done in sound checks, especially on the Spirit Tour over in Australia, like the first month of it. She was

> **How many 1.5 liter bottles of water does Jewel drink each day?**
>
> At least five

If you were stranded on a desert island, what CDs would you want with you?

My favorite CD, I would say, is Ella Fitzgerald's *Cole Porter Songbook*. I would say, some Etta James, Elvis, Rolling Stones, Hendrix, Edith Piaf, Nina Simone, something by Schubert.

This is a hard question because I don't really listen to a lot of music. When I am it's just to study it. Study people's phrasing, or what chord they're using under what melody. It's usually just studying. I've been that way for a long time. It's how I taught myself to sing. I was always stopping, rewinding, stopping, rewinding, to see how they did it and to see if I could do it.

On an island I'd probably prefer to read. The characters seem like they would at least keep me company.

whipping out really strange things during the sound checks. There were songs that were like 18 minutes long that would be these incredible stories—totally improvisational.

Shane We didn't have TV and we rarely listened to radio. Pretty much the only music shows we went to when we were growing up were either our parents' shows or festivals where they were performing.

We're not, either one of us, people who like to be out there among party-goers. I'll put it this way: Believe me, there are hillbillies in Alaska and she's one of them. It's in her blood. She can't help it. I think she's a very simple person in terms of what she needs in life. She's very serious about her relationship; they just kind of stay on this ranch in Texas. She's a very simple person with very complex ideas and thoughts. A very intelligent person and yet she needs only simple things in her life.

One of the great things about her, one of the things I really like about her, is that she doesn't know a lot about the world. You know what I mean by that? She doesn't keep up with who was on *Entertainment*

SHE'S a stand-up GAL.

Tonight last week, or whatever. You can mention a movie or a director or, frankly, a song, and she might not know what you're talking about. In that sense, yeah, I think it's kept her sheltered, because I think she's a little bit afraid of the world in that way. I think she probably stays inside herself because of that. But because of it, there are brilliant songs written and she thinks a lot.

She's a stand-up gal. From the first time I saw her, and heard her records and stuff, I just knew she was a force to be reckoned with. I think she's one of the best songwriters around. I've always admired her honesty. That's one of the great things about her — she's very honest. She's got some kind of magic or power and it just comes through. People notice it.

Billy Bob Thornton

Stuart It's cool because when you're not around a lot of stuff you just have to draw from your surroundings and yourself. I think that's how she got her sound, just by doing it by herself for so long.

Lee She really didn't have a lot of outside influences when she was growing up. She didn't know the whole roster of modern music. She had no idea, I think, what, like, Madonna was. So the songs she would sing—the ones she made up—were just so fresh because they weren't that influenced. It was her own thing.

Recording Session, Nashville, TN, 7/11/01

Steve We were introducing her to all sorts of stuff on the road. We'd buy her CDs. And she'd listen to everything. It was a totally new experience for her.

If your house was burning down and you could only grab one thing, what would it be?

It would definitely be all my writing books—the journals. There are like 20 of them now. A big stack. I've always decorated them with pictures or paintings I was into at the time. Some are leather-bound and they're all different. They're really eclectic, really beautiful to see a stack of them. That and one of my guitars. The blue one. And I have some jewelry I want to get out. [laughter] And some bras and panties will surely be worth the effort! [more laughter]

Doug I gave her the *Sticky Fingers* CD, and she had never heard it before. I lost that one to her. I lent her U2's *Achtung Baby*, and I haven't seen that one again. And Hendrix.

Like an hour before the show, we'd all hang out backstage and just crank up the Hendrix or the Stones and get ready for the show. It was fun to watch someone who had never heard the music—the great stuff. And she'd be freaking out about how good it was. The next day or two, she'd come up with a song that was inspired by that stuff. You could hear the Hendrix or the Keith Richards influence coming through in her newer rock writing.

What common snack food does Jewel dislike?

ice cream

CONSTANTLY creating

Atz Lee When she was younger and she was just writing songs, before stardom had struck, it was just more jotting in journals and writing with guitar chords and finding a voice. And it was just talking about stuff going on in her life at the time. So, of course, once you actually come at it as a career and you make one album and then another, your style of writing is going to be completely changed. It's mainly in her professionalism now.

Before, the songs would just lead her, and she would kind of uncover something. She would just fully expose them, and they would become a song.

Now she can come from the other, more professional end and come up with an idea and have a really strong idea of what she wants to do with the song. She goes into a lot of different levels now, and so her music is becoming more evolved.

Monty I think there are essentially two types of songwriters. There are those that are inspired to write by something, whether it's an experience they've had during the day or a melody that comes into their head. And then there are other people that are "Okay, I've got to write a song today." And they'll sit down with a guitar and a pencil, and they'll muck about until stuff starts to come out. Jewel is very much an inspired writer. And she's very prolific.

Alan If, for criteria, you're considering just the songs that Jewel has written, either by herself or in collaboration, that are finished songs that she performed, it's like in that 400 range. But like, as an archive manager, I'm interested in everything that she's done and any song that she's performed. Even if it's a cover song. And there were many songs from the early days, like when touring with her dad and things like that. If you're including all of that, there's probably twice as many.

Recording Studio, Nashville, TN, 7/11/01

Bibi   She always has a pen in her hand. She's a maid's worst nightmare. She never seems to have enough paper, so she'll just write on sheets. We'll leave a hotel room, and she'll have a whole song or poem or a drawing, or phone numbers, written on the pillowcases and sheets. There are probably sheets all across this country that have original material by Jewel on them.

Lenedra   Jewel is prolific. She's constantly creating, but not just songs or music. She switches to different kinds of expression so that she's always working at a very high level of engagement. So when she exhausts herself in one area of creativity, it seems that another area really comes forward. Over the years I've seen Jewel always to be involved in one or more modes of creativity. I've never seen her when she was not involved. Right after her last record, she did no writing but she started painting madly. She did many portraits. And then after a time of that she began writing poetry again, but stayed away from songwriting completely.

At one time, what junk food was Jewel hooked on?

Jelly Bellies

After touring with Jewel a few times it all made sense: just exactly how all those rock stars, with their money and fame and seemingly awesome lives, ended up overdosing or becoming washed up after one album. It seems to me that being a rock star on tour is the hardest path through temptation. Anything you want can be yours. Upon arriving at a gig, you are shown to your dressing room and asked if you need anything. There would always be some food and drink and then that offer for anything else. Nobody ever says what "anything" might be, but it sounded to me like some people really meant *anything*.

In the dressing room, I would hang out and talk to the roadies—guys that have been in the biz for a long time and worked with everyone—and I'd hear their stories about the parties and the drugs and how great the life of a rock star was. It soon became apparent to me that being a rock star seemed more hazardous to your health than crabbing in the Bering Sea of Alaska.

That's when I realized how truly unique my sister was. After the gig was done, everyone would start to party—everyone except Jewel. It was a rare night that she would decide to go out with the band, and when she did, it was not the usual scene. I mean, not a lot of rock stars drink whiskey and water without the whiskey. Most of the time she would simply go back to her hotel room and stay up till 4:00 in the morning writing new songs—most of the time alone.

In the end, that's what being on the road is all about—devoting all of your energy to the music and the fans. At times it gets so intense that the challenge becomes just finishing one show, let alone trying not to get overwhelmed with the fact that there are 200 to go before you get to go home for your three days off, only to start it all again. There are a lot of musicians in the world, but it takes a certain focus to make a positive impact and keep your passion strong and pure in those kinds of circumstances. Jewel has a number of ways to keep it together and get the job done and, as you'll see, a lot of good people around her to help deliver one of the best live music experiences to ever hit the road.

Atz Lee Kilcher

Stephen When she taps into why she's there, it's magic. When she steps onstage and the light hits her, it's magic. It's kind of awe-inspiring when you see it. Because everything is all built up to that one point—all the interviews, all the traveling, the plane, train and bus tours. You get that this is what she's there for—being onstage.

The greatest quality for a singer to have is identifiability. That when she sings, you know who it is. The generic-sounding singer, where you really can't tell who it is—of which there are many right now (I mean, I have pretty good ears and I can't tell them apart)—she's not one of those. She has an extremely unique sound. She's very talented in that her control of voice is pretty extraordinary. She's very emotional. She's very theatrical. She's very intimate. She delivers her ideas better than anyone else could. And you know it's her.

Musically, I think she can go a lot of places. She has tremendous ears and she can hear into much heavier harmonic content, chord-wise. She can hear deeper into those things. Even some of the things that she writes that weren't on *Spirit*, or other things—you know, she's not confined by any sort of stereotypes about what it should or shouldn't

She's ᴀ **one-off,** YOU KNOW?

be. So sometimes, because of odd tunings, and just searching it out and looking for something interesting, she finds some colors that are extremely deep. They're not two-chord mentality folk songs. They're not folk songs. There's some very deep harmonic stuff going on. That gives you the indication that you could go as deep as you wanted to go, and that as long as she heard it enough to be comfortable with it, she can find her way into just about anything. She is a singular artist. She's a one-off, you know? I work with people who are brilliant, talented people sometimes. But they're not one-offs. They're kind of one of a breed that seems to be running through the industry at a given time. A type of artist, or a type of singer, or a type of voice. And she's not any of those. There's one Jewel.

Patrick Leonard

Doug We rehearsed for about a week before going out, and I never really heard her doing solo stuff. We played our first show in Paris. It was a pretty small club, and she sang two songs before we even started. I was just knocked out. There are only a few people that could almost drive me to tears. Not necessarily because it's a sad song, but just the beauty of the voice. It was pretty amazing.

Mark Her voice is so versatile. She can sound like a young opera singer and then sound like a Steven Tyler if she wants to.

Sharon I studied voice, so I have a real appreciation for the purity of her voice. The tone and the frequency are so pure and strong. I stand backstage and listen and I have tears. And if I have tears, I can imagine what that voice is doing to people in the audience, who are getting her full attention.

I've seen people come backstage and say to her, "You've changed my life." Her voice carries that healing frequency.

Couldn't your stage show use some choreography and hydraulic lifts, strobe lights, dry ice, harnesses and pulleys?

I'm no dancer and as for the hydraulic lifts, strobe lights, dry ice, harnesses and pulleys—those things should remain in the bedroom.

from the HERS start

Steve She has such a presence onstage. There's a point in the show where she does three or four numbers by herself. The audience usually gets really, really quiet and sits there and listens intensely.

Trey She doesn't need us, man. Her with just her guitar is amazing. I mean, it scares us. We don't want her to do too many things with just her guitar.

West She's always grateful that people come out and spend their hard-earned money to hear her sing.

Mark She just wants to go out there and play her songs for them. She just wants to play.

Steve There were one or two nights during the Spirit Tour where she really had to pull out all the stops, you know. Especially at the end, she would just do one encore after the other and just really win them over, even though they were hers from the start.

Rehearsal, This Way Tour, Tampa, FL, 6/13/02

Brandon I remember one time Jewel was playing this venue in Houston. It was a shed, so about a quarter of the people who paid the extra money were covered. But the other 75 percent were out in the grass. It was a large venue, there were about 12,000 people there.

It was really hot, really humid. It's Texas, right? We're hanging out as Steve Poltz is about to go onstage. And Jewel's chilling as this huge thunderstorm comes over and just starts pelting rain, like Texas rain. It's coming down so fast and so hard, and the thing is, it's a really hot day. The water's coming down so fast it can't even run off the streets. Most of the crowd is out there sitting in the rain, waiting for Jewel.

I didn't have anything to do at the moment, so I started running around in the downpour, taking my clothes off, and I'm running around in my shorts. It was really fun. Huge raindrops. It was biblical, this storm coming down on those poor people out there.

So I go and I get Jewel. She sees me running around, having a blast. And she's like, "Oh, I'm in that!" So she runs outside and she rolls up her pants, and she's in some T-shirt, and we're running around getting completely drenched. This is all backstage.

What's funny is she just shot this music video for a song, so she has these extensions in her hair. So this water is just pounding her hair and the extensions start coming out. She's got these big chunks of hair falling, and the color gets all weird and she's like a wreck. She's just running around sopping wet.

Then she said, "Let's go onstage."

So she just runs onstage in the middle of Poltz's set, sopping wet, dragging me. I've never been in front of more than a classroom-size of people. She starts dancing around, running in circles, being completely silly. Poltz just kind of flows with it. He thinks it's cool. He starts playing this square dance, swing-your-partner-round-and-round thing. So me and Jewel and Brady are all running around the stage, spinning each other around. Acting silly right in the middle of Poltz's set in front of 12,000 people. She runs and grabs the mic and yells her condolences to all the people in the rain. I think it kind of made the people who shelled out their 20 bucks feel a little bit better.

MIXING it UP

What bores you to death?

Anything that's the same for too long. I like growing, changing and learning. I like changes of scenery. I hate things being overexplained. I hate reading the same kinds of books. I'm very mercurial. Just a real Gemini.

Doug   I've played with a lot of people that stick right with it, every night, the same set. But Jewel mixes it up, which makes it nice. It's not so robotic.

You know, she'd come in that day with a song, and we'd learn it at sound check and play it that night. And that was really exciting. You never knew what was going to happen.

Steve She would just give us the structure, as far as those new songs go, and just let the band play. It was great freedom for us. Usually, when you have an artist like that, they want to dictate every single point, as far as what you're going to play and how they want the song to sound.

Trey A lot of people don't want you to add your colors. That's another difference with her: She hires guys because she likes their playing. She's not scared to let herself be surrounded by those types of players.

When the opportunity came, Atlantic—especially [then vice-president and general manager] Ron Shapiro—said, "Would you like to work with Jewel doing a Christmas album?" I jumped at it because she's a fabulous singer. But then, working with her, I discovered many other wonderful things about her. First of all, she has so much in reserve. This young lady can sing an "Ave Maria" without a vibrato, like an angel. She can sing "Go Tell It on the Mountain" like an Appalachian gospel. And so on.

So this was a wonderful, wonderful experience for me. In fact, and I did tell her, that album would be one of the albums I would take on a desert island.

When she came into the studio, it was like 96 degrees outside. We had Christmas decorations, in the middle of July, in the vocal booth. And she was a professional. But I wouldn't even call it just profes-sional. She was a creator—extreme energy and inner instinct.

Then I realized, when promoting the album on television shows, live, out there in the rain in front of Rockefeller Center, she wouldn't be afraid of changing the melody, or going up to another level, singing a high note. Being that it's live TV, usually people are more cautious. This young lady would take all these chances and land on both feet. A true artist! Her range covers many styles. In this Christmas album, I was astonished. She'd do a song in Latin, then an extremely happy and joyful "Winter Wonderland," which borders on kind of jazzy phrasing, too. This lady has such a wide range, she can do anything she wants. She'll do whatever's natural for her. She's not an artificial person, to choose things in order to be hip or something. She'll do whatever's right for her.

Arif Mardin

> She was a **creator—EXTREME ENERGY** and **inner instinct.**

Monty She always performs in sync with the crowd. It's kind of like the tide coming in and going out. The way the shows go is a bit like the tide coming in on a beach. She kind of moves with it. She's a real great gauge for working an audience.

Mark   She doesn't want things to get predictable. That takes a little getting used to for a lot of players, because most tours you do have the same set for six months.

This Way Tour, Wantagh, NY, 6/22/02

Stuart   It shows that she's in tune with the moment. If you feel different some night, you probably won't want to sing that song just right then. And there's probably a reason for it. I dig that. It keeps you on your toes.

Alan   Quiet, respectful audiences tend to get really interesting set lists. She's more daring when people are paying attention, and she just gets into it more. I've noticed that when crowds are rude and really noisy, the set lists are more generic. The more attentive and respectful the crowd, the more experimental and adventurous she'll be.

Atz Lee   There have been lots of tears over the years. Hopefully there are a couple of good friends near. She calls me a lot—we kind of talk a lot—and other family members. There's a small group of people helping support. Basically, she carries the brunt of the load and very rarely gets shaken, but when she does there's a team surrounding her, sending her love. Everybody has a certain level of understanding and spirituality towards each other, so that even if months go by and you don't know where Jewel is or what she's doing, the phone can ring and she can call up and say, "I'm in Baltimore and I just had the worst show of my life, and this psycho guy jumped on the stage and said that I was supposed to marry him, and the security guard that was supposed to save me wanted my autograph . . ." And she can just kind of go off, and you can be there for her and be understanding without needing the specifics of what she's been doing.

This Way Tour, Tampa, FL, 6/14/02

Sharon When traveling, we decided to make every hotel room as much like home as possible. Because when you're traveling, it can get pretty hard living in those impersonal places night after night. So one thing we did is bring her own blankets and pillows. We would go in and strip the bed and on would come her own.

But at one hotel, we got in late and I went up to the room to set things up. But when I get there I find that there's no bed. There's just this enormous table, like you'd find in a boardroom. So I go back down and I find Monty and say, "There's no bed in there."

Jewel's sleeping on the bus still; it's like 3:00 in the morning.

And he says, "What do you mean there's no bed?"

I take him in and show him: There's no bed.

And so the hotel says, "We have another room." They take us down to this other room, and it's a smoking room. It's just reeking of cigarette smoke. We go back to the other room, which has a huge conference table in the middle of it. And Monty said, "Alright. Let's move this table out of here, we're going to move the bed in."

So while Jewel was still sleeping on the bus, we get bus people up and baggage people, and we literally take down a table—a big long conference table that seats about 30 people. We move it, taking off the legs, lifting it down and out into the hallway. And from a room across—a nonsmoking room—we take the whole bed. And we get it all set up and we make her bed and then we go down and get her. Mind you, we have four or five people

Which rock legend provided the studio for recording the non-live tracks of *Pieces of You*?

Neil Young

What country do you really love to visit?

I enjoy Australia a lot. If it wasn't so far away I'd be there a lot more. It's great. The people are great. They're like Canadians, but there's more of a criminal element, which is fun. [laughter] They're really tough. The cowboys that come from there are super tough. And the place, it's sort of like what California must have been like 50 years ago. There's a lot of pretty country. I love it. Really friendly people. And in Melbourne, it's really arts-driven.

How have you learned to pace yourself in the accelerated world that is modern music?

I do well being able to come and go, because I know I don't always have to be available and be the Kewpie doll that's always talking about herself and smiling. When I know it's for a finite time, like a four-week stretch, I do pretty well. Because I'm able to get away for what I need — and get back to the writing, to the quiet. So that kind of rhythm works really well for me, and it's really benefited my run on this record. You can't be on all the time. I can't.

working on this, including Monty and myself. We brought her in, tucked her in, and she went right back to sleep.

Come morning time we find out the room next door was supposed to be hers. The hotel just didn't tell us. All we had to do was open the door.

For what movie soundtrack did Jewel record Donovan's "Sunshine Superman"?

I Shot Andy Warhol

Darren Yeah, besides all of the rigors of performing four to five nights a week, putting on a good show, traveling by bus, never really stopping for too long, not to mention the work that she is creating, there are also the security risks. As with any popular female performer, there's a certain percentage of obsessive fans—fans that want more than just an autograph. It's people like this that can make it hard for Jewel to just walk alone from the bus to the catering area, or from the dressing room to the stage.

Sharon You're always watching other people. We never let Jewel off the bus first. Going into a hotel, somebody always goes before her.

Brady I had to do this sound check thing for *The Horse Whisperer* for Steve Earle, so I brought Jewel over to the studio with me just to hang out. She dug that, and I said, "We're going out later—there's this blues joint—to see this band play, so if you want to go . . ." And I think at the time she had had like death threats or something from the Lilith Fair. There was some weird thing going on with some security. So she had this bodyguard, and he was all buggin' out about us kinda takin' her into Nashville unaccompanied. And I'm like, I opened up my trunk, showed him my stuff (I ain't gonna say what I had, but you know, there was a little artillery in the trunk), and I'm like, "I think we're covered on that end." And he was like, "Okay, fine."

that SILENT TIME

Stephen   The nature of this business is such that people are always coming at her with requests and things that would slip through the cracks. "Oh, we forgot

This Way Tour, Cleveland, OH, 7/7/02

When touring, do you have a chance to really get to know all those places you visit?

I made it a habit, when I was traveling, to pick up a novel, a play and a short story by a local talent, like when I was in Ireland. That was a really great way to sample the culture, because it's so hard to get out to a museum when you're moving around so much.

to ask you this and could you do this. You're in this city now, and it's the only opportunity you'll have." And it's a constant state of turmoil, if one allows themselves to believe that you have to do all these things.

This Way Tour, Fort Lauderdale, FL, 6/15/02

Brandon   She looks forward to quiet time and prayer. She's very introspective and she loves to write about her thoughts.

Monty   She acquired a great love of afternoon tea. Quite often, on the road, especially on a day off, she would be very interested in finding out where she could go to sit and relax and have afternoon tea. It's become a staple now on the road.

Sharon   Every day she has like two hours of silent time, of meditation time.

Whenever we could get her to a park, she would go walking. It's hard to get to that natural place when you're on the road. She would always try to take that silent time for herself.

Steve   The Spirit Tour was a tough haul, especially toward the end. All those 14-hour days, no weekends off. She was pretty wasted. She had to do interviews every day and the concert every night. It wears on you. I know, I went through it a little bit in the '80s, with Mister Mister. When you're in a band it's easier, because you can kind of pass it off to one of the other guys. But when you're a single artist like her, it's very, very difficult to do that every single day on the road.

Stephen   I've seen her struggle with, "What's the right thing?" Her dedication to her fan base and to her music and to herself—which one does she put on hold to make a decision?

Brandon   When you're constantly in front of thousands of people, and doing these meet-and-greets, and doing five to six shows a week, it's hard on your voice.

Stephen   I don't think the voice works unless the mind is working well—you know, unless your head is in the right place.

Lenedra   Neil Young once gave her some advice that helped her loosen up for the show. Early in her career, she opened for him at Madison Square Garden. She was so nervous before the show, but he came back to her dressing room and did such a gracious job of putting her at ease. He said to her: "It's just another hash house on the road to success. Show them no respect." [laughter]

Sharon   I don't think people have any idea what she does to prepare herself before she performs. She sits alone and goes inside herself. In doing that, she brings all of herself in, together, to give the best she can for those who are watching. Part of that I think is a

What's the best thing you ever spent your money on?

Lots of things. There's a lingerie shop in Paris that's just . . . ah . . . exquisite! Beautiful stuff!

Money can be really great. Buying my horse was great. Doing Higher Ground for Humanity is great. The ClearWater Project. Buying a really good steak when you're starving. It's really relative to your desires at the time, so it could be anything.

responsibility, an obligation that she feels, and I don't believe all performers believe that.

Bibi   Another way she stays balanced is to get out and do things. I remember her first time in Europe. Every city that we were in, we went out. We checked out the sights. We found like little farmers' markets and little town fairs. I remember buying scarves in Germany, in Bremen, in the little Renaissance fair they had set up in the beautiful old town. I remember buying hand-dyed scarves, things like that. We always got out and saw the city.

She also liked to read a lot. She was always reading, backstage, in airports, driving in the car—all the time.

The reason I like being her friend is that, before we met, I sort of had this idea of her being this delicate, waifish folksinger. We met and she's smart and funny, boisterous and bawdy. She has an expansive character. And she's told me some of the nastiest jokes I've ever heard in my entire life. She has possibly the blackest, most twisted sense of humor of anybody I know. And that's saying a lot—I have friends that work on The Simpsons. I know some twisted people. This woman that everyone perceives as being this delicate, sensitive, New Age woman swears like a sailor and tells me jokes that would make Eminem blush.

If she was some prepackaged, choreographed pop star, I really wouldn't have an interest in being her friend. But, you know, she's a very multifaceted, complicated woman. She's smart. She's insightful. Very wickedly and disturbingly funny. The funny thing—I have to keep going back to this contrast—you'd think

VERY **wickedly** and **disturbingly funny.**

that someone who maybe just listened to her [first two] records or just has an idea of her as a public figure would think that if you said—I don't know—the word fuck in her presence, she'd either start crying or force you to leave the room. And the truth is, she swears like the kids in South Park. She would fit with those characters like a charm. I really think most people don't have any idea about that side of her personality.

In all honesty, she's one of the most remarkable musicians I've ever met. I remember one time she was doing a Bob Dylan cover with Garth Brooks. And they were working at this studio around the corner from my house. So she called me up and I went down to visit. When she was done working, we were in the live room, where they did the recording, we were just playing around. I was playing piano and she was singing. And, yeah, musically, the way her mind works, I think she's very, very gifted.

Moby

Shane   When she reads a book she gets really introverted. And I know when she

64

This Way Tour, Pittsburgh, PA, 6/29/02

was on tour, she was sitting around going, "Damn." Kicking herself, biting at her lip. And I said, "What's up?"

She said, "I was reading."

She gets so into it, gets quiet and not in the mood to put on a show, so she has to be careful.

runningCAPERS

Brady   I just like having a lot of fun when I'm on the road, you know, doing stuff, stealing golf carts, riding motorcycles and stuff, that's just what I like to do. So I would go kidnap her, and we would run capers around like every fairground and stuff. It was fun.

Brandon   Sometimes she liked to go out with Poltz and the band, people that she's

What's a joke you've tried that really fell flat?

Once, onstage in Germany, I was telling that pot story about going to Mexico with Steve, and nobody was laughing. People usually laugh, but there it was just dead. And I was telling them about the long drive with Steve and how I kept asking him, "Are we there yet?" Until finally he said, "Goddammit, no!" And I acted like he hit me, thinking it would be so preposterous that people would laugh. But I just heard like a collective gasp. They were horrified. It just bombed. It really sucked.

continued on page 67

really comfortable with. But I don't think she likes to go out a whole lot.

Bibi The other night, she was like, "Damn, I wish it was Saturday." I was like, "Why? What could we do on Saturday that we can't do on Sunday?" It surprised me because she never wants to go out. But that night she wanted to be around people, watch them, because she's on her own so much.

So we went to this drag queen bar. It was such a dive. It smelled like stale beer. It had a really bad drag show. It took them forever, and there were only two tables of people there and us. Of course, everyone recognized her.

They did the little drag show and then the host asked if anyone had any jokes, if anyone wanted to tell jokes. A few people got up there and told jokes. Then Jewel got up there and told a joke and it was such a dumb joke, and everyone knew who she was so it had a weird effect, which is what she thought was funnier than the actual joke. To her, that was the joke. She has a weird sense of humor like that.

The actual joke that night was "Why do girls wear perfume and makeup? Because they stink and they're ugly." It's supposed to be funny because it's so stupid, and because Jewel was telling it, people just looked at her and said, "Whaaaat?"

It didn't go over very well. I think people were kind of uncomfortable. [laughter] They were kind of confused. So we left, but she had another joke. And she wanted to go back and tell it to kind of redeem herself. The joke was even worse. It was REALLY bad. I encouraged her not to go back.

Which Jewel song did Merle Haggard identify as his favorite?

"Pieces Of You"

Monty   She went through that phase of going out with the *Spirit* band when we were in Australia. They were all still getting to know each other and having fun. For her, it was the first experience where she was going to be working consistently on the road with the same bunch of guys. They would go out and say, "Jewel, do you want to come with us?" And for a while she was going off and hanging out with them. They would even go into a club, and if there was some band gear on the stage, they would get up and play—you know, sit in. She would get up and sing as well.

Steve   There was one night, in Australia, where we all went out as a band to a club. And we ended up sitting in and Jewel sang "Summertime." It's something she wanted to do, and Tony, the bass player, knew it and I knew it and so we just went up there and winged it. It just blew everybody away. Nobody thought that Jewel had that range of style. She can sing anything, really.

Brady   There's a place called The Lakeside Lounge in Alphabet City. And so we hang out drinking there and stuff. I've got some friends that own the place. We're rollin' in New York so everybody wants to go downtown, wanting to go out. We went down to Lakeside and there was a band playing. They were just finishing, so we were like, "Yo, can we sit in?" They were like, "Sure." So they had all the instruments we needed, and we played for about an hour. Oh yeah, it was packed out! People coming in off the street. You know, they were walking by, and 'cause there's a display window, there's people looking in like, "What the hell?"

continued from page 66

But it made Steve giggle. So I went farther into the story and got this whole bit going about how he became this really abusive person and I was cowering from him. And I looked back, and Steve was on the floor trying not to pee his pants because people were so disgusted with the idea of their little Jewel being abused.

What band backed Jewel on a 1995 Conan O'Brien Show?

Counting Crows

West It's usually pretty fun on the road. It's like a family environment. Maybe that's something she carries with her from Alaska, that sort of interest in family bonding, that sort of familiarity that she establishes when she wants to get to know people.

Steve We'd go out, rent bikes. It was like a little family. To be in tight quarters like that for a year, you gotta get along, help each other out.

Stuart She wants to hang out. It probably gets a little tedious doing all the interviews by yourself. When she sees us, she seems to light up, like, "Hey! What's going on? What are you guys doing? Let's go do something. Let's hang out." That's real refreshing.

Brady I remember one time we were outside of Chicago or something, you know. I said, "Yo, let's get this golf cart, let's go check out this place!" You know, we didn't want to walk around so we just stole the cart, and one of the employees was just, like, boned out. It was great, we just split, just left. Rollin' everywhere.

Which role did Jewel perform for the stage?

Dorothy (in The Wizard of Oz)

"What's she really like though?"
"Does she eat meat?"
"Does her wiggly tooth really wiggle?"
People want to know my sister—they want to know the person living behind the music. At times, fielding these questions as her brother has proven to be as entertaining as being the celebrity. But the bottom-line truth is this: Jewel is just trying to be everything she dreamed of as a child. The fact is, her childhood dreams didn't involve piles of money and screaming fans. More so, she wanted to be graceful, intelligent and honest; true to herself and all things around her. She possessed a certain drive to just simply become herself instead of trying to become like the things around her.

The only person who can truly know the real Jewel is Jewel herself. So as I sat writing this introduction, I decided to try calling her and asking her what she thought about it all. It was strange to call my sister and ask her about her feelings regarding who she really is, beyond what people think she is.

I wanted to go straight to the source, so I called her magic cell phone number and found her in Nashville recording *This Way*. After we caught up on each other's lives, I jokingly asked her, "So, who is the real Jewel?" After all, can any of us answer this about ourselves? She responded by saying how she felt her public image seemed to be more serious and professional, while hanging out with friends she definitely became more whimsical and silly. She also said that most people don't realize how hard she is on herself, how overly judgmental she is regarding her music as well as her own life. "I task myself quite tremendously," she said. "I have high standards for myself and sometimes push myself too far. I'm not very forgiving of myself."

The people around her every day know her best. These two qualities she described for me are things observed by those close to her and touched on in the following chapter. And there's lots more. They provide pieces of the puzzle, such as her habits and preferences, and by combining their perspectives we can start to see the person behind the voice, the music, the image: the real Jewel.

Atz Lee Kilcher

Brandon I never really thought of her as a rock star, and I still really don't. She's just someone who loves what she's doing.

Does your wiggly tooth really wiggle, as the name of your publishing company suggests?

Nope. It doesn't. I called it wiggly tooth because it was a really nice way to say "snaggletooth." Cuter. It's like "potbelly" versus "fat." Huge difference.

"Standing Still" Video Shoot, Agua Dulce, CA, 8/29–30/01

Lenedra She has done a great job of staying focused on the music. She just needed to see that it could be done. Working with Merle Haggard was something that Jewel really benefited from, because he knows how to keep the music industry in perspective. He doesn't get caught up in all the show biz or industry distractions. He told her to do the same, saying, "It's all about the music."

Atz Lee She's really just staying true to herself and what she likes and what she enjoys. She's just living her life. That's how she creates her image, by not jumping right into one.

Steve The day that I auditioned for the band, I found out afterwards that I got the gig, and I was just hanging out in the studio and I called my daughter and told her that I got the gig. She was very excited. So I was on the phone with my daughter, and Jewel was around, so I asked Jewel if she would say hello to my daughter. And without hesitation she said, "Of course I will." And that's just the kind of person she is—she was like that throughout the tour. She's very down-to-earth and sweet and, of course, talented. She ended up talking to my daughter for a few minutes, and I was really impressed with that. She took the time to do that even though she had just met me.

Jewel is someone who wants to be comfortable wherever she goes. She comes from such humble beginnings, and honest beginnings, that the world of fashion, in all its insincerity and foolishness, is just not for her. It's like the emperor's new clothes. She can spot insincerity a mile away and knows it when put on her, knows it when it's being done. She tries to find truth, her truth. And sometimes that's not what other people have in mind about the way they want her to look, to market or sell or promote her.

The one thing Jewel knows more than anyone, and her fans know, is that the words she sings, her thoughts, her feelings, matter a hell of a lot more than a designer dress. If that's what she's basing her career on—how she looked, her hair, her makeup—then it wouldn't be Jewel. That's someone else. There are people who have entire careers based on their look. And they have wonderful voice coaches who help them almost hit the right notes, then they have machines that tweak it, and they lip-synch when they sing. And they have writers that write the music for them, and all they do is show up on the music video. That's what the public is buying—that package. With Jewel, the public is buying her truth. And it's so remarkable and so extraordinary that all the packaging and marketing in the world can't create it.

She TRIES to FIND **truth,** HER TRUTH.

Kevyn Aucoin

Mark I told her she's too normal to be a superstar. She needs to start acting a little weirder. I don't know, be meaner. [laughter]

She's just so down-to-earth compared to a lot of superstars you run into. Doesn't have the weirdness about people being around or meeting friends of yours. She's just cool. I mean anybody who's going to date a cowboy has got to be down-to-earth.

Trey She's like a sister that I haven't seen for years and we're just trying to catch up—she makes you that comfortable.

Brady One thing that I've always noticed is that when we go shopping, you know, she'll buy a couple of pieces that maybe cost a lot of money, you know, but she always thinks about it. She just doesn't go out with, "Oh, I want this," you know what I mean? She's always pretty simple, practical, about the things that she wants. And I think that's a very good trait. Usually people think superstars go out and buy whatever, you know what I mean? She's like really, you know, good about her business—smart about it.

Bibi Now that Jewel's famous, it's kind of awkward. If we go out with a group, she'll pick up the tab. But if it's just she and I, sometimes she'll pick it up. But I feel like I'm taking advantage of her—I don't do that with my other friends. So occasionally I'll pick up the tab as a gesture, saying, "You don't always have to do it."

The girl can't figure out tips at all. She can't figure out how to do it. She told me this story: She went out to dinner with a bunch of people, and it was like a few hundred dollars, so she couldn't figure out the tip. So she went to the bathroom to figure it out. And then came back and wrote it out.

West She has these little quirks that make her so real. That's what people respond to. She's like us.

Trey She's just really, really, really normal.

Brandon She doesn't care what people think of her appearance. She just walks around in sweats and a T-shirt and her hair's a mess, and she doesn't really care. She's confident.

Lee She doesn't mind getting dirty. She can come from having a facial, where they're putting $300-an-ounce creams on her face, and really not care. The next thing, she comes back and her Armani pants are trashed and full of horsehair. She goes from one to the other without thinking. There was a time when I would just shake my head and laugh. All these designer clothes covered with horsehair.

Bibi One thing that I really love about Jewel is that, when she gets dressed, every day for her is like dress-up. She doesn't just throw on jeans and a T-shirt like the rest of us. I've seen her put on like ten different outfits. And they'll be the weirdest combinations of things you've ever seen. She'll put on hiking boots with a pair of jogging pants with a Hawaiian skirt with a scarf wrapped around it with a hooded sweatshirt over that and big sunglasses, and then she'll put on makeup and then she'll usually take it all off and put on jeans and a T-shirt. She's always playing dress-up. She's like a little kid.

Lenedra The transparent dress at the Grammys was a complete surprise. In the hotel room, in regular light, it had a body stocking and slip underneath the sheer part, and nothing risqué was visible. But when she got to the photography room at the Grammys, the backlighting, the frontlighting, all the flashing bulbs, all combined to make the dress really transparent. In the photos in the newspaper the next day, Jewel was very surprised to see how revealing the photo was. Especially when the dress, in the hotel, seemed almost excessively modest, compared to what other girls were wearing.

When filming *Ride With the Devil*, what did director Ang Lee have Jewel do to develop her acting?

Tai Chi.

Stephen When I first saw her, I was struck by how larger-than-life she looks onstage—meaning big in performance terms—but she's just this little bitty thing, this little beautiful entity. But she just comes off as this powerhouse woman onstage. The difference between the two is just amazing to me.

Lee She's this great feminine influence. Then she'll put on this Cartier watch and ride a horse and get it all scratched up as she moves bales of hay around.

Darren I remember when she got pretty upset once—I think she was serious—when they airbrushed her photo and fixed her teeth in a newspaper article. She was making jokes about it, and then she went on this whole thing about how she should do an ad campaign for Crest with her uncorrected teeth. She just turned it into jokes like that.

Atz Lee The media, they need to have a really limited focus. Their focus can only zone in on so many people or things at once. Jewel isn't concerned when the focus isn't on her. She's not out there to change old headlines, or to prove something wrong. Or say, "I'll show you and go out and do what you said I couldn't do." Or even try to get in the headlines when she isn't.

She's just going about her life. Sometimes that media focus falls upon her, and wherever she's at with her life right then, that's what you get to see. And it comes and goes. That's kind of an image in itself that perhaps people enjoy because it's somewhat more original and honest.

Brandon Jewel's always been so excited about trying to experience what God is to her.

Does spirituality really play an important role in your life?

It's weird to hear people talk about my spirituality. It's a very private thing to me. Not a practice or a religion. It just is. I didn't know other people were so aware of it in me. I don't talk about it ever, really, though I have to agree that it is at the root of all I do. But being irascible and irreverent fit into it for me, too.

"Standing Still" Video Shoot, Agua Dulce, CA, 8/29–30/01

Sharon Her authenticity stems from this really solid spiritual center that she's in touch with. I also think having many different facets is the nature of pure creativity. To think we can only be one thing, and for those facets to be not as pure and authentic, isn't recognizing the spiritual identity at the core. If you can find that spark inside yourself, everything you do from there will be authentic; everything will be pure.

Lee   Spirituality is at the core of her existence. Everything she does—trust me—is connected with her spirit. I know she has a very deep faith and it will rule what she does.

Sharon   It's not like a hat that she takes on and off. It's not a role that she plays. It is what she is and who she is. I hear people say all the time, "I'm trying to be more spiritual." And they already are a spiritual being. Jewel knows that she is a spiritual being—it's that special light inside her. So she's not searching outside of herself somewhere; it's already inside.

Stephen   What she does is a spiritual thing. It touches people's lives and their hearts.

Shane   She really does want to do something good for people, and that desire is rooted in her spirituality.

Lenedra   Jewel's spirituality is a very personal matter to her. It's most visible in her relationship to nature and her commitment to understanding and challenging herself to live her values.

Brady   Her soul and her spirit as a person, I think, are her best assets, you know, 'cause she can be just sweet as hell.

selfless ACTS
of **kindness**

West   Jewel is all about giving people opportunity. Because she knows better than anyone else how hard it is to get a break. Especially in this business. She helps people. I remember when she took me to dinner for my birthday, and she asked me to come on board full-time. She made me the offer to leave my job. And I had a great job at the time, but it became apparent that this was the time to move—that this was a once-in-a-lifetime opportunity. And that's what Lenedra and Jewel are all about.

Lee   She wants to see her friends do well. I'm one of those who she has really reached out to, to give me a better place in this world. She's done the same for a whole bunch of people.

Atz Lee   We've always been really strong on the spiritual side in dealing with people, trying to give the same level of respect to the bus driver that you do your boss. I think that's really strong in all of us. I think that really helped when she went to build, when she went to make the team of the people she has around her, she had all that inside her. When she went to choose people, she had all that in her and she went looking with a standard. A lot of musicians seem to get into it, and they don't really have a standard of what they want for a manager, or what they want for employees. They're not really concerned with that; they just want to make their next album. So she spent a long time thinking about who she wanted. She was saying, "I want somebody I can really trust and who's going to be working as hard for these principles as I am."

That's what brought together the people in the company and gets incorporated into the music. And the ClearWater Project, Higher Ground for Humanity and Soul City Cafe are all built upon that basic respect for humanity.

I was playing at a place, Java Joe's, in Poway. I went in there and I was just going to play. It was kind of like a hangout. Java Joe's has always been a place where all the musicians hang out, even if you didn't have a gig. We'd play poker in there and mostly play our music.

Jewel was waitressing there, and my throat was just shot from singing too many shows with the Rugburns. So I asked her if she could make me something for my throat and she made me some sort of concoction. I don't know what it was — some herbal thing. I don't really drink that crap, you know? Something natural and healthy. So we started talking and we hit it off. We got along really well. We started talking about music and songwriting, and I remember she asked how she could get a following like the Rugburns had. I told her to play the same place every week, like every Thursday night find a place she can play and make it her own. And so she found that place at the InnerChange.

When she started playing at the InnerChange,

Certain people just have that FACTOR: the IT factor.

there would be 5 people there. Next week, 10. Next week, 20. Certain people just have that factor: the It factor. So she was making like a ton of money, and I don't think she even had a bank account. Not a ton, but she was making good money there. It was all cash. I think she used to stuff it under the mattress or something.

So I had like thousands of dollars of parking tickets. I was constantly getting parking tickets because I would ignore all parking laws. It got to the point that I didn't even care anymore. I would just illegally park, thinking, "What does it matter?" I had so many tickets. And one day I walked out of the house and my car wasn't there. I thought, "Oh my God, my car was stolen." So I called the police and it turns out it was towed. Because of all the tickets. I must have had about $1,200 worth of parking tickets. So I couldn't get to a gig, and she had this cash stashed away. And she just gave me it, even though she was still living in her van at the time. She got the money, gave me it, said, "Here, take this."

Steve Poltz

Lee She has realized where she has gotten herself. She doesn't really need much for her own happiness. I mean, she's giving up a lot of her own money for this. She could be someone who just made a couple of million and says, "There's my ranch." There's this ranch she wants to buy, and I've seen her put it off a bunch of times. It's more important right now that the money goes to support the ClearWater Project. Or just that the monies are kept in check with her original goals.

It's not just a bunch of bull to her. Higher Ground for Humanity—it was a goal of hers.

Alan The EDAs did a lot of amazing things and many of them were selfless acts of kindness. A perfect example of this happened in 1997. Every year the EDAs tried to come up with some idea for Jewel's birthday, and rather than give her gifts, cards and these types of things, they showed that they understand where she's coming from by going out and helping people in their own community.

So on Jewel's twenty-third birthday, in 1997, rather than give gifts to her, the EDAs encouraged each other to find a way to effect positive change in the world. That year, the entire EDA list organized to help a severely injured hit-and-run victim named James. He was a San Diego man who had no medical insurance, and he was in need of a van outfitted with one of those special lifts so he could go back to work. So what the EDAs did is raise money to help buy a lift for this van so James could accomplish his goals. It was a perfect example of EDA generosity. What was also very cool is that they didn't just raise money. They actually took it further than that: Several of them became friends with James. They picked him up and took him to Padres games and brought him down to Java Joe's for shows. They brought that whole thing to the level of friendship, which I think is a much cooler thing than just saying, "Here's the money." That was an amazing thing. It was a perfect example to show they understood where she was coming from.

Lee She really wants to see people elevate. She knows that one of the best things for humanity is that everyone evolves. If you help someone evolve in some kind of way, it's a domino effect. It all will add up in ways that you maybe don't even expect. Who knows what could come out of it—other things that make you happy.

> **Which video was filmed at the same soundstage as Gone with the Wind?**
>
> "Down So Long"

Brandon She's pretty conscientious about what she puts in her body: She doesn't drink or smoke. She's pretty clean when it comes to consumption.

Lenedra When Jewel did the *Wizard of Oz in Concert*, a number of the actors took her under their wings and gave her a lot of support. Debra Winger was very sweet and helpful with Jewel's nerves just before going onstage.

Jackson Browne, in a very paternal way, kept an eye on Jewel and helped her get her bearings with the performance and in that world in general. At one point during a rehearsal, the room was very chilly. He saw that Jewel was cold so he handed her his shirt, which he was wearing over a turtleneck. So she wore it around that day and gave it back to him.

The next morning, he came to her and gave her a very odd lecture about not using drugs. She said, "Okay, but I don't use drugs."

He said, "Jewel, you can be straight with me."

"No really. I don't use drugs."

But he went on to tell her that he had learned that drugs are a really bad idea and she shouldn't get started with them at all. Put together with the music business, it was an unbelievably bad idea. She said he was very fatherly about it, but the whole thing was a bit strange.

The next day I realized what had happened. I said to Jewel, "Oh my gosh, you know what it was? You remember when you were wearing his shirt and you came to me and you said you had a headache. And I gave you two of the powdered aspirin that are in the little folded-up packets?" She started laughing, realizing that he must have thought that these little powdered packets were cocaine.

Later that afternoon when we got in the limo with him, I handed Jewel one of those packets. He was shocked. I offered him one and he was just so alarmed. Then Jewel and I burst out laughing and told him it was aspirin powder. His face turned red.

He said, "You know, I thought it was coke, and I thought Jewel was doing it. I was so concerned that I took it to a friend of mine, and I said I found this in the pocket of the shirt Jewel was wearing." He told us that the friend took it and stuck some of it on his tongue and said, "Well, if she is doing coke, it's really bad stuff."

> **What movie soundtrack featured a remix of "Foolish Games"?**
> *Batman & Robin*

Shane Because of the homestead, we kind of had a philosophy—or, at least, I did—"If you, yourself, can't grow it or kill it, don't eat it." I think there's a real respect, a real understanding, of what life is. That's what living on the homestead was—seeing a different way of life from the city. How detached people can be, only vaguely knowing where milk comes from. Or where meat comes from.

When you got famous did you stop eating middle-class foods, like peanut butter and fast food?

"This Way" Video Shoot, Los Angeles, CA, 8/28/02

West One time we were walking down Prospect, and there was this cigar store there. She said, "Yeah! I really want to try one." She's really health-conscious, so this was totally out of character for her. So she went in there and got, I guess, a real quality one, whatever one they suggested. So she took a few puffs on it, walking down the street, and she just turned green.

[laughter] No, I'm probably eating more of it because I'm on the road all the time. I'm eating fast food all the time. You know, I get done late. Even if I'm rodeoing with Ty, we'll get done late and end up eating at a KFC at midnight.

As my health has gotten better, I've gotten a lot higher tolerance to those kinds of foods. When I was living in my car, I wasn't able to tolerate a lot of foods, and I'd get sick a lot because of my kidneys.

Lee   On tour, I would keep track of what she ate. I have this color thing going on with food. So there's a certain balance, like, when she needs yellow vegetables. I tried to keep her balanced, making sure she ate things that are [laughter] all colors of the rainbow. Making sure she got a lot of greens and oranges. She loves good food.

---

*T*immy's a term I came with up for my a-hole. We were always traveling, and we didn't want to be crude around other people because there are always runners. You know what runners are? They're people who work for the promoters. They go get things. Like, "Oh my God, we don't have any guitar strings. Send a runner to get it." You know, they're always some cool kids. But we realized the bigger Jewel got, the more people are looking to get things to gossip columnists. You know what I mean? They wait like jackals. I could never do that—have that level of spotlight. It's like, damn!

So one day, because we're always eating weird food in so many different countries, I said, "Well, Timmy didn't like that meal."

They WAIT LIKE JACKALS.

And Jewel and everybody's like, "Who's Timmy?"

And I said, "Timmy's my a-hole." They started laughing so hard. Brady spit his drink out. He started running with it all the time: "Uh, Timmy didn't like that at all."

We'd be at a full meal with promoters and everything and we'd be like, "Do you think Timmy's going to like this meal?" The promoters had no clue.

Jewel would be like, "Timmy didn't like that at all." She'd be talking about it. She'd be signing autographs and turn around and say, "Timmy's not very happy about that last meal." We made her call hers Tammy. She never really went with that, she wanted to call it Timmy.

Steve Poltz

Bibi   Jewel and I have this thing: We call each other Sushi Sluts. We want to have these satin jackets made, kind of like Pinky Tuscadero, satin jackets, with our names, but fake names, embroidered on them. And these Asian women holding pieces of sushi, these really buxom women with whips and whatever, embroidered on them. That's how we see ourselves—as Sushi Sluts, because every time she's in town we go out for sushi. We love sushi.

Lee   She eats according to what she's doing. She'll eat just vegetables for a while and then have this feeling and say, "Okay, I need meat."

Stephen   She's wise enough to know what it takes to ensure her instrument is in tip-top shape and what it takes to do what she does. She's very clear that she's the one in control of her life.

Doug   She's like one of the dudes.

T-Bone   I tell you what, I've worked with quite a few females and I've had some great relationships with them. But none of them has been one of the guys more than Jewel. She actually gets a bit irritated when she feels like she's not spending enough time with us. She can hold her own in a room of men at any given time.

Brady   Totally! She's like one of the boys—it's like we're hanging out, kicking it. She likes motorcycles, too. One particular night, my friend's got this nice low rider, big Harley, you know, a real nice one. So we drove over to the hotel, and I was going to bring Jewel to the show on the back, just for a cruise, just to change it up that day. Everybody was freaking out! Promoters and all that other stuff.

     The only person that was cool about it was her mom. Her mom was like, "She grew up riding horses and motorcycles, she's fine." So we rode it to the gig and after the gig, we get offstage, we're rolling out and she jumps back on the bike and there's kinda like a little drizzle. But we're rolling out and it's funny 'cause we drive down this alley and all these people mob us. So we had a couple of security guards there, but she signed autographs sitting on the back of the bike, you know. Until she got tired and hit me on the shoulder. "VARrrroom," I hit it and we were gone, off into the Sydney night.

Doug   She hawks the biggest loogies.

Darren   She'll sit there and talk with me or whoever and, in the middle of her sentences, just spit like a cowboy. Just spit on the ground. She's kind of like a tomboy that way.

Don't you ever hang out with girls? You're always with guys.

I don't have very many girlfriends. My mom's always been such a good friend, and she's a real solid chick. There's none of that whiny do-you-like-me kind of chick stuff that drives me up the wall. And none of the cattiness—I just can't stand all of that. [laughter]

     Actually, I have some girlfriends that I like, but like any of my friends—we're not in touch all that frequently. I was raised around men. So it's never been an issue. I can deal with men. And it's also just my job. I mean, there just aren't many women in on the job. In terms of being on the road, you're not going to find many women on the crew or in the band. It's percentages more than anything.

Brady I love it when she spits at me onstage 'cause she's like a little punk rock chick or something. A big ol' loogie. Or she'd give me the bird sometimes, you know—I dig that. We did this thing with our hands: We shape it like an L if something's really lewd or somebody does something really bad. Or somebody messed up onstage and you know like whoever. If it was me, I'd point at Tony or I'd point at Steve George, point at her even. I get a kick out of that.

I was in her room at the Mercer Hotel. She and I were exchanging jokes, and Tracey Ullman had recently told me some jokes. I just thought they should talk because they have that great sense of humor. So I called up Tracey and told her I was with Jewel, and I gave the phone to Jewel to tell her a joke. She told Tracey a joke. And Tracey's response was "That's sick." Now, Tracey and I have watched videotapes of things that are so mad and insane, of just public access TV moments—crazy, off-the-wall stuff. And her show is not exactly mainstream humor. I was so sure this joke was going to fly, but it just didn't happen. It just goes to show that you can never count on anything.

"That's sick."

So she grossed out Tracey Ullman, which is saying a lot.

You know, when you're not racist or homophobic or misogynistic or anything of those things, you can make jokes. Because what you're making jokes about are the people who think that way. You're not making jokes about the subject. You're laughing at the mind that would conceive that as being humorous. You go beyond the joke and into the absurdity. In other words, *South Park*. Or *Strangers with Candy*, another favorite. It's sort of equal opportunity offensiveness. It levels the playing field and makes everyone the same. Comedy's a great leveler.

Kevyn Aucoin

Lee She's so much a girl. But she was brought up in what some people might call a masculine environment—hardworking. She really understands a lot of what makes a man operate. There's no mystery for her. She's not some Southern belle who will sit there and wonder, "Why does a man do what a man will do?" She sees what drives them.

god, what a **TOUGH** chick

Brandon Her intelligence carries over in her humor and in her ability to tell you what's up if you're messing around. One time, during the tour, I was just flirting around with some girls, so she called me over and read me the riot act, made me see the light. [laughter] Nothing serious. She just called me a punk in a few different ways.

Bibi   She's not the kind of person to take just anything from anybody. She asks questions of the people around her, the people she works with, for example. She'll want to know why things happen the way they do, why you're doing something, and she definitely stays on top of it. And if you're not on top of it, and you don't have a quick answer, she'll give you hell for it.

T-Bone   You have to be on your toes. The thing with Jewel is, even if you don't know her that well, she will come off in a way that has you saying, "How do I take this? Do I throw a punch at her or what?" I've learned to recognize that she's just going to be her, at any given time, with anyone. That's the best thing because you know what you're getting.

Stuart   She definitely likes to have a verbal bout with anyone at any moment. That's cool. She's messed with me. Like I had red hair when I first met her, just full-on red hair. Then I saw her a few weeks later somewhere else and she's like, "Oh, wow, you dyed your hair back. Well, you're fired." Like the hair was the only cool thing I had to offer.

Mark   I've got sarcasm coming out of my pores, and she's worse.

T-Bone   If you don't know her, she can come out with some very offensive things, just joking around. But the thing I look for isn't what you say, but what you're about. Her heart is in the right place to me, but it's easy to get the wrong idea about her because she comes on so strong.

Mark   I'm surprised she hasn't got more bad write-ups from just joking around like she does with interviewers. Because when it's written in black and white, sometimes you don't get the delivery, or that it's a joke at all, and you just come off sounding

Do you consider yourself to be an especially demanding person to be around?

I'm quite opinionated and I'm not really afraid to speak my mind, and so often I find that I'm wrong. But I've never felt particularly prideful about admitting it. I do demand a lot from myself, and I demand it from people around me, too. It's probably not all fun for them.

like an a-hole. I'm surprised that she dodges as many bullets as she does.

Stephen She can handle herself quite well—this is a cowgirl at heart.

What is it about your jokes that some people find so potentially offensive?

For some reason I really love to, as the Brits say, "take the piss." You know, mess with people. I know people expect me to be demure and kind, so sometimes, just to play with people, I'll say something really redneck, very seriously, just to see them stutter. It's amusing and it breaks the ice, usually. Once they get I'm joking.

"This Way" Video Shoot, Los Angeles, CA, 8/28/02

Lee Around 1990, I was doing commercial fishing, and I overheard these guys on a boat talking about this young Kilcher girl. This was before I had met her. They were making bets on who could have sex with her. It just freaked me out. I thought, "This poor girl." She must have been about 16 or 17 at the time. So I was driving down the street once and I picked her up hitchhiking and I said, "Listen, you need to look out. Someone's going to mess with you."

She had this knife in her boot and she pulled it out and said, "Would you mess with me?" I was like, "This girl is hot. She can take care of herself."

That was when I said, I want to know her. She's my kind of friend—a strong, take-care-of-yourself personality. God, what a tough chick. And then, when I got to know her, she just became more and more intriguing. What a great mix. She's the sweetest person I know—and I'm not just saying that—and she's also the toughest.

Brandon Jewel's very street-smart. She lived a harsh lifestyle in years past, so she knows the way things work. She knows what's going on. You can't pull a quick one on her like she's some innocent kid from Alaska. She's traveled all around. She's hitchhiked. She was singing in bars with all sorts of guys hitting on her all the time. She knows how to take care of herself. She learned pretty quick, from an early age, traveling and performing in bars. I think she witnessed a lot of that bar kind of lifestyle—what people do for money, what people do for success, what people do for love.

the **beauty** of NATURE

Bibi Usually when she's home in the afternoon, she likes to ride her horse.

Lee Mostly, she has a couple of good friends. She doesn't like wasting time at all. When you're young and growing up here, you don't have a lot of time to just do nothing. I think that's really helped her in the whole celebrity world she lives in. She knows what it is to be busy. And what it does: It keeps your mind superactive.

Lenedra I've noticed that the thing she needs to stay engaged in her art is time away from people. She needs a break from everyone: family, friends, fans. And time in nature. That seems to be the thing that fuels her most.

Brady The most fun I've ever had hanging out with her was like, we were in Sydney, Australia. I think two or three times we went to this park. I forgot the name of the park now but it was right on Sydney Harbor, and I think that was some of the most relaxing times 'cause, you know, we were in one place for a week instead of getting on a plane or bus the next day, and it was just kinda cool. So, you know,

What video features Jewel and Steve Poltz?

"You Were Meant for Me"

What would you be doing if you weren't a songwriter?

I'd just live a creative life. I feel like, if I were a mom, for example, if I had kids at this point, it would be a creative process for me. Life as artwork, you know. I don't feel particularly caught up in which form it takes. Just creation in general. That's the gift of being human—we can create. We know God through our ability to create. It's a divine right and as sacred as the model of the universe.

continued on page 87

we would meet up in the lobby and then we would roll out to this park and we stayed there for hours. I remember one time in particular we couldn't find like a taxi, we didn't have a van, we couldn't get in touch with anybody, so we were just like hanging out in this park for hours all day. But it was great, we were just sitting, you know. Really not saying nothing, just sitting, looking at the sky, at the ducks, the flowers, just sitting on the rocks looking at the water. I think that's one of my fondest memories of seeing her and how she just digs being in nature, you know. I could see that she was at one with it, you know what I mean?

Lee   Truly, she's the happiest when she's walking with the wind blowing on her. She's really a true lover of the beauty of nature. The wind, the water, the earth under her feet—those things really make her happy. I think if she lost all her status now, if it went away or whatever, she could end up being happy just being on a farm somewhere, where she could absorb the natural element.

DIFFERENT
EACH**time**

Sharon   An appetite for learning is why she has so many facets: She writes, she paints, she sings. It fuels the creative drive, and she's always doing what she can to reinvent herself.

Atz Lee   She changes. When the media focuses in on her from month to month, she's a different person each time. People find that interesting, because she's not concerned about all these things that most people are.

Lee   She evolves quickly. So who knows where she is right now. That's something that's always made me happy: seeing her change and evolve.

Shane   The most elusive aspect to being famous is really

how public opinion is created. A couple of things have really come to represent her. It's not like she is consciously representing herself as being a home-stead-raised, homeless-living-in-my-car, naïve-cute-blonde-singing girl. But in an interview, you mention that you lived in a car for a while and that's how you're portrayed forever. People latch on to that.

Steve She's got a lot of different sides to her—that's what makes her so interesting.

Brady I think that she's pretty direct onstage, though, so if anybody's ever gone to a show they'll know that she's funny, she's tough, sweet. She's all these different emotions rolled up into one thing.

continued from page 86

There are a lot of things I'd like to do. I'd love to study science. I've toyed around with taking the bar exam. Not with the intent to practice, but just for the education that would come with it. Or study economics. I'm really fascinated with how things work — the mechanics. That's all a kind of creativity.

"Break Me" Video Shoot, Los Angeles, CA, 3/12/02

Lenedra Jewel is a very complex individual and artist. Her personality has as many expressions as her art, which is why she enjoys being involved in many different kinds of expression: music, writing poetry and prose, acting and the visual arts. She gets to express from different aspects of herself.

People always ask me if fame has changed Jewel. Of course it has, because all experiences change us. That's how life works. With Jewel, the focus has been on being conscious of, and crafting, the changes. The changes that I've seen primarily are those concerning the development of her artistry. Her increasing awareness of her gifts results in confidence and maturity in the way she works and the art she creates. And all of it is informed by a growing understanding of the larger world—and being at peace with it. In gradually becoming a participant in that larger, global world, Jewel's range and depth as an artist continue to grow. Because of that connection between herself and the world around her, Jewel will always be a creative person, reflecting both the complex and simple truths of the world around her.

She is who I hoped she would be, personally. It's not an act. I guess that was the pleasant surprise. You kind of always have expectations for that, but many times you tend to get let down, because the persona doesn't match the image. It did and I was pleasantly surprised. She's not precious about anything. She's not precious about microphones, gear, about having to have only blue M&Ms in the candy bowl and candles. None of those things. The only thing Jewel insists on is lunch when she wants it. And that's it. And don't let the blood sugar go down too low or she'll bail on you.

She is bound to individuality, and that's what I think is the strongest point in who she is. I really enjoy that fact. She's not trying to be someone she's not. And when she senses it, she really shies away from it. She's very tough on herself vocally and writing wise. She goes through some swings on both of them. Every day.

She is bound TO INDIVIDUALITY . . .

Berating herself every day. I think it's a love/hate thing. She just gets down on her singing, if she doesn't get it right away. I think she has a very low tolerance for flopping around. She likes to get to it.

I think, in this day and age when there's so much cookie-cutter stuff going on, she's her own deal. I think she could be doing this a long, long time. But she's also the kind of person that I wouldn't be surprised, just because of knowing who she is, if she one day just said, "I'm tired of this. Next."

I think she would do this whether or not she made any money. I think the word artist is overused in the entertainment community. I think there are a lot of entertainers, musicians, but when you say artist, I think she is an artist. And name five artists that are in the pop scene right now. You'd be very hard-pressed. I think that would be my highest compliment—she's an artist.

Dann Huff